Galina's Hope

Beyond the Fire

By Galina Loseva Messmer
as told byBrenda Noel and Dawn Sherill-Porter

WESTBOW
PRESS®
A DIVISION OF THOMAS NELSON
& ZONDERVAN

Scripture taken from the New King James Version. Copyright © 1979, 1980, 1982 by Thomas Nelson, Inc. Used by permission. All rights reserved.

All Scripture quotations in this publications are from The Message. Copyright © by Eugene H. Peterson 1993, 1994, 1995, 1996, 2000, 2001, 2002. Used by permission of NavPress Publishing Group.

WestBow Press books may be ordered through booksellers or by contacting:

WestBow Press
A Division of Thomas Nelson & Zondervan
1663 Liberty Drive
Bloomington, IN 47403
www.westbowpress.com
1 (866) 928-1240

ISBN: 978-1-5127-0401-3 (sc)
ISBN: 978-1-5127-0402-0 (hc)
ISBN: 978-1-5127-0400-6 (e)

Library of Congress Control Number: 2015912150

Print information available on the last page.

WestBow Press rev. date: 9/23 /2015

This book is dedicated to the memory
of our beloved Peter, Alexander, Alexey, Dennis and Elsie

Acknowledgments

Most importantly, my utmost praise and thankfulness to my Heavenly Father, who has bestowed His Grace upon me through my darkest hours. Next, I would like to thank my loving husband Peter for all his perseverance helping me to organize my thoughts and writings over the years. It was a challenging task that included a stirring trip to Russia and many long conversations sorting through feelings and memories. Peter also composed a number of passages of the manuscript and spent endless hours preparing it for publication. For Peter and Elsie's children, Eva, Steven, Joshua, and Jesse, I want to express my most heartfelt love and appreciation for the wonderful blessing of being able to raise them as my own children; even while their own precious mother Elsie is with my dearest boys in heaven. I look forward so much to meeting her some day in glory. A heartfelt thank you to all of our extended family, who have been by our side for many years, both during and after the tragedies. Many of them have been mentioned throughout the text of our story and words cannot express our gratitude for all they have done to help and support us. I also want to thank Maria and Lena Isupov for their dedicated help in translating my original manuscript from Russian to English. My special thanks to Brenda and Dawn for their hard work, insightfulness, sensitivity, and faith that resulted in the crafting of my writings into a final form. They put their hearts into what was a tearful task at times. Finally, I would like to thank everyone at Westbow Press for all their hard work and creativity.

Introduction

I am Galina. The years of my life have taken me from the frozen lands of northwestern Russia to the beautiful shores of the Black Sea; from the western coast of the United States to the natural wonders of upstate New York. Each stop along my journey has left embers of life in my heart—some kindle joy, some burn with remembered pain. But, no matter what has occurred as I have traveled my life's path, I have found reason to rejoice. For what is joy when pain is never known?

My current home is located in the Finger Lakes region of upstate New York, not far from Niagara Falls. Referred to as one of the natural wonders of the world, the falls serve to remind me of the greatest wonder—the great goodness of my God. Gazing at the splendor of God's creation, I am continually reminded of a hymn we sang often in my homeland of Russia—*How Great Thou Art*. In Russian, the words ring with power: "*Great God! When I look upon this world, on everything you have so beautifully created, by the power of your hand. I see all the creatures to whom you give the light and take care of with your Father's love. Then sings my soul; how great Thou art.*"

It is fitting for that particular song to resonate with my spirit. The poet, Carl Boberg, was inspired to pen these lines when a violent thunderstorm descended on a radiant afternoon. The majestic power of approaching, broiling clouds filled with lightning and thunder, coupled with a magnificent, sun-drenched day, caused words of glory and praise to rise in his heart. The poem was later set to the tune of a folksong from his homeland. I, too, have witnessed the radiance to be found within God's world and experienced the virulent storms that rage, bringing winds of trouble and torrents of sorrow. I, too, have been awestruck by the power of my

God displayed even within the sometimes-violent events of life. And my story is also set to the music of my homeland—the heart bond that ties me forever to the land of my birth. There is a Russian expression: "There lays buried my umbilical cord." The love for my country and the nostalgia I feel for my homeland will ever be a part of me. It is like a melody that plays in the background of all events of my life.

The title of this book is based on a theme that seems to play throughout my life. Hope is ever before me, though often through life, hopelessness threatened to drag me into the dark caverns of despair. As so often happens as we walk with the Lord, He provided some incredible object lessons to help me realize how imperative it is that hope remains alive in my heart.

God's Word tells us in Hebrews 10:23: "Let us hold unswervingly to the hope we profess, for he who promised is faithful." Within these life-altering words lies the powerful truth that has taken me from ashes to beauty, from sorrow to rejoicing, from weakness to strength, from death to life. I do not tell my story to bring renown to my own life; I tell my story for it is His story—the story of how my loving Lord Jesus orchestrated my life for my good, and hopefully, for the benefit of all His church.

Chapter One

Focus on Hope

I was born on February 1, 1962, the fifth child in a family that would grow to include eleven children—six girls and five boys. Hardworking and loving, my parents, Alexander and Galina Titar, raised their family in Cold War Russia. It was an atheistic, communist land that was deficient in opportunity, especially for those

> Philippians 4:8
> "Finally, brethren, whatever things are true, whatever things are noble, whatever things are just, whatever things are pure, whatever things are lovely, whatever things are of good report, if there is any virtue and if there is anything praiseworthy—meditate on these things" (NKJV).

who refused to join the Communist Party—the ruling class who determined the state of existence for everyone within the borders of the Union of Soviet Socialist Republics (USSR). From youth, we were steeped in communism, beginning with the Pioneers (a mandatory youth program at school) and culminating with the expected choice of each student to join the Communist Party.

The city of my birth was Saint Petersburg in the northwest of Russia. However, my earliest memories are of Petrodvoretz, a small city situated just west of Saint Petersburg. The snow-covered, wind-whipped winters there were long; it sometimes seemed warmth had deserted us forever. Winter days were extremely short—the sun lighted our way for only six or seven hours a day.

Spring would eventually arrive; along with it came lush greenery and the vibrant colors of flowers and gardens filled with delectable fruits and vegetables. In northwestern Russia, fresh fruits and vegetables were true delicacies, because the growing season lasted such a short time.

My father was amazing. He was a handsome, jovial, mountain of a man and my best friend. He had a great sense of humor; fairly often, my brothers and sisters and I would laugh at my father's wit until our insides complained. Dad worked long hours as a plumber and in various factories when I was very small. It was hard work, but Dad never complained. The money he earned barely covered the necessities for his large family. So he often took on side jobs to make ends meet. For many years, in addition to holding down a full-time job, my father studied chemical engineering in the hope of improving the lives of his family. In pursuing his degree, he made periodic trips to the university in Moscow. When he returned, he would often bring back special gifts for us: Moroccan oranges, bananas, and pineapples. These fruits were not your average grocery store staples. They were really something extraordinary, especially for children who rarely feasted on such exotic food.

Although studying engineering while working left little time for him to interact with us, somehow, Dad always found time for us. When I was a teenager, my father worked as a control room operator for a large oil refinery. He finally earned his chemical engineering degree only to find that an engineering position would pay less than a blue-collar position. This was not happenstance either. In the Soviet Union, many professionals earned less than laborers as a matter of communist ideology. So my father's dreams of working as an engineer died, but his good humor and strong faith remained untouched.

My mother, Galina, was a serious-minded woman. Having lost her father through divorce at a very young age, she suffered from this pain for most of her life. Her mother, Antonina Nikolaiyevna, had been a battlefield nurse in World War II. During those violent, frightening years of the "great patriotic war," my mother and her brother, Anatoly, were sent away to the Ural Mountains for safety just before the Germans blockaded Leningrad (Saint Petersburg was renamed Leningrad by the communists). Grandma Antonina remained throughout the 900 day siege that followed. During the winter months, supplies were brought into Leningrad by way of a vast network of ice roads that crossed the southern end of Lake Ladoga and terminated on its eastern shore which remained under the control of Soviet forces. Collectively, these roads became known as the "Road of Life". One of Grandma's first assignments was at a medical outpost on the ice roads. It was very dangerous, for the roads were continuously hit by German artillery and bombs. Later she was transferred to an army unit during the offensive that finally broke through German lines and fought all the way to Berlin. She received several medals for her heroic military service.

Mom and her brother Anatoly were not reunited with their mother until several years after the war. Lacking both a mother and a father for a good portion of her life, and surviving many terrible things during the war, caused my mother to be a very reserved, unemotional woman. Though she may not have been demonstrative, none of us kids ever doubted her love for us. She was a very devoted mother, and under her care, we never felt deprived in any way.

My parents, though very different in temperament, shared one overriding bond. Both loved the Lord above all else. I remember so well the meetings at our church in Saint Petersburg. It was called Pocloniya Gora, which means "Worship Mountain." It was the only registered Baptist church in the city at the time. (During my childhood, churches had to be registered with the state. Any church that did not do so was illegal.) Prayer, praise, and joyous fellowship rang throughout the sanctuary; it sometimes seemed we would praise our way directly into the very presence of our Lord. Life was to be lived to the glory of God; this was taught to me from the time I can remember, and for many years, I never considered there could be any other way. Meeting with other believers was simply the way of life for the Titar family. And a glorious way of life it was! We shared our lives and our possessions. But most of all, we shared the love of our Lord.

It's strange, looking back, that I never thought of us as poor. When we lived in Petrodvoretz, there were ten of us crammed into a small, two- or three-bedroom apartment. Later, when we moved into Leningrad, the housing authority gave us two adjoining apartments with a total of four bedrooms, but in Petrodvoretz, life together with my family seemed peaceful and happy in those few hundred square feet. To my child's eyes, all was right in my world. The simplest of pleasures are things I still remember. Each little toy or the tiniest piece of candy filled me with joy and gratitude.

Some of my fondest memories are of our entire family attending circus performances a couple of times each year. However, the experience was much different from attending a circus today. In Russia at the time, everyone dressed in their finest attire to attend such a grand event. I recall vividly my mother and father leading the way toward the colorful entrance. Daddy would take turns putting the younger children up on his shoulders. When it was my turn, I felt so very special perched high above the rest of the crowd. Daddy was big and strong, and to me, he was the very symbol of love and safety. I can still hear him call me Galychka, his pet name for me. Oh, how I admired my father!

As a young child in the 1960s, I wasn't aware of the manipulative, controlling tactics of the communist agenda. I didn't know Christians faced persecution and harassment. I didn't know how they were often denied promotions into management positions. And I was unaware that many were imprisoned and some still lost their lives for their faith in Christ. I was only vaguely aware that the majority of the folks among whom we lived did not believe in God because they had adopted the atheistic, Communist doctrine. At least while I was little, my parents managed to shield me and my siblings from the dark and oppressive side of the socialist society that they navigated daily.

When I was a child our nation was only a couple decades past the time of Stalin. During Stalin's reign of terror people who were devout in faith and outspoken, easily drew the attention of the KGB (the state police). Yet, because of the long history and influence of Christianity, particularly the Orthodox Church in Russia, the Soviet Union never actually instituted laws against it. None the less, it was considered superstition and even subversive to the goals of communism which included striving for utopia on earth, without God of course. During my parents and grandparents generation evangelical churches were watched closely and most were shut down or went underground. Witnessing publically to others about the price Jesus paid for our freedom from sin and death was almost a certain invitation for a visit from the KGB. Many Christians were among the millions of people abducted and hauled away by the state police to face fabricated charges (since religion was never actually outlawed). This usually involved some convenient and false allegation about something that was illegal, such as vagrancy or stealing state property. The next step was usually torture until the unfortunate victim signed a false confession with the typical result being an eight or ten year sentence in the gulag (the state run system of concentration camps) with its unspeakable atrocities. Many of the labor camps were in north Russia or Siberia and conditions were so bad that this was very often a death sentence. Another common fate was outright execution at the hands of the secret police.

Every family in Russia was affected by the violent revolution of 1917 and the subsequent horror of Lenin and Stalin, sometimes referred to as "red terror". Lenin organized his radical communist party among the ranks of dissatisfied workers in the cities, poor peasant farmers, and angry, disenfranchised soldiers from the battle lines of World War I. The target of their malcontent became the wealthy and members of the ruling class of Russia whom they sought to overthrow. My maternal great grandfather, Nikolai Myagkov, was a member of the aristocracy who owned a large estate and mansion. He was abducted by an angry mob of Bolsheviks (the common name for Lenin's radical communist party) who tortured him badly and he died shortly thereafter. My great grandmother, my grandmother Antonina and her sister Maria were then forced into a life of destitution and poverty in Leningrad.

Sometime after World War II, my paternal grandfather Nikolai was arrested and sentenced to ten years in the gulag for stealing a bag of potatoes to feed his starving family. Fortunately, when Stalin died he was set free before his health completely failed. By the time I was born the gulag had been dismantled and Stalin's reign of terror was over, but some political dissidents and outspoken people of religious faith were still being sent to prison for years at a time under the Khrushchev and Brezhnev regimes. Pastors, members of unregistered "underground" churches, believers who produced or circulated Christian literature, or young men who didn't want to serve as soldiers because of their Christian faith are examples of those who were particularly vulnerable when I was growing up. Another favorite tactic was to commit Christians to insane asylums under the guise that anyone foolish enough to believe in God must be crazy.

In addition to being expected to give up religious freedom, every citizen was encouraged to be atheistic and given ample opportunity to become a Communist Party member. In order to join the party, it was expected that one would promote atheistic propaganda. This propaganda was everywhere, from the workplace to the schoolhouse. Though it may sound a contradiction in terms, atheism was the state religion. It was a hopeless nonbelief system upon which the government was built and operated. Everyone must have some constant to cling to in life. For the Soviet Union, that constant was communism and its ideology of utopia on earth.

My family was unapologetically and devotedly Christian. Harassment of my family by the KGB began in Saint Petersburg when I was only about five or six years old. It started because my father, Alexander, recognized the futility of a life anchored in the quicksand of atheism. He was willing to challenge it and let his faith shine forth in the spiritual darkness rather than hide it. (Jesus exhorts us to do exactly this in Matthew 5:15.)

One day, my father was called into an all-employee meeting at the factory where he worked. The speaker was a state official whose job was to motivate and manipulate people toward greater patriotism to the communistic creed. My father listened as the speaker sang the praises of communism. At one point, the speaker said, "God does not exist. If God does exist, why does he allow sorrow, suffering, wars, death, and sickness? If, in fact, he does exist, then he must be a blood-thirsty, vengeful, hateful god." Following his rant against belief in God, the speaker asked if anyone had any questions. My father raised his hand.

My father walked with purpose to the front of the auditorium. In a strong, steady voice, he proclaimed, "This speaker is wrong!" He explained that, indeed, God does exist and He is a God of pure and unlimited love. He raised his voice to a multitude of people who lived without hope of eternal life and quoted John 3:16: "For God so loved the world that He gave His only begotten Son, that whoever believes in Him should not perish but have everlasting life" (NKJV).

The audience of workers sat in stunned disbelief as my father's words filled the auditorium; all present were well aware that such a speech would be reported to the KGB. Speaking out as my father had was a major affront to the communists. Faith was tolerated only in prescribed places at prescribed times, such as services in state registered churches. It was never to be spoken of in public, and certainly, not in a communist propaganda meeting! My father was very aware of the possible repercussions of his actions; knowingly, he had set himself up as a target for the KGB and their state-enforced consequences. But fear of man could not stop my father from living out the Great Commission to go and tell the truth of the gospel.

As we were to find out in the years that followed my father's public confession of faith, he became a marked man. Although he kept the details from us at the time, the KGB began to hound him, spying on his every move. However, my father was known as a hard-working, respectful employee. He had received recognition and accolades for his superior work ethic and attitude. His photo even hung on the factory wall as an example to other employees of excellence in the workplace. It is most likely because of his excellent work record that the authorities did not arrest him on the spot; a more insidious tactic would be employed.

Because of the ever-present KGB and because my father thought the warmer climate of his childhood home would be better for his family, he decided to move south to Krasnodar, where his parents lived. It was a place of abundant warmth and sunshine (much like the southern states of South Carolina or Georgia in the U.S.) located in southern Russia on the banks of the river Kuban, just east of the Black Sea. Of course, the KGB had the power to follow anyone anywhere and they followed my father to Krasnodar where the surveillance and harassment continued. My father didn't tell us many details about what was happening to him; but he couldn't hide it when the secret police finally contacted him shortly after our move. My father was ordered to meet KGB agents in a certain park not far from the local KGB.

Ironically, my father later acquired an apartment in a building situated right behind the KGB. I lived there for a short time as a young woman. I could look out my apartment windows and see the barred windows of the state police building across the courtyard. I have since come to know, from the writings of Aleksandr Solzhenitsyn, in his work titled the Gulag Archipelago, the Krasnodar KGB was very brutal and murdered hundreds of people in the basement of their headquarters during the height of Stalin's purges (the killing of all those perceived to stand in the way of the communist party). I shudder now to think that probably happened in the very building I lived next to.

The night before my father was to meet the KGB agents our family was filled with fear and anxiety. We prayed and spent time together for what we feared would be the last time. The next day, my father slowly walked into that park alone. Though he feared for his life, he already had his mind made up about what he was going to say.

The KGB men promised my father a huge salary and a long list of benefits if he would do one of two things: either publically denounce his faith on television, or become a secret spy inside the church. They promised him a large house or apartment, a nice car, and all the food and clothing his family would ever need. There would be no more hunger or want. Being a loving father who wanted to provide adequately for his family, this temptation must have been difficult to resist.

In response, my father bravely told the KGB agents the story of Jacob and Esau. He explained how Esau had given his inheritance over to his brother for a bowl of stew. He stated he would not be like Esau; he would not betray his birthright as a child of God in exchange for temporary treasures. He refused to deny his faith in the Lord and give up his eternal inheritance in heaven.

Furious, the KGB agents leveled more threats against him and his family. However, God must have enacted a miracle for they simply let him go! He walked out of that park and returned safely home. My father continued to live the Great Commission and even served as an elder in the church. While it is reasonable to suppose the KGB continued to watch him, he was never again approached by them.

Something else quite amazing happened as well: the Lord provided the very things the state used to tempt my father away from his faith. I was reminded of Jesus' words: "Therefore I say to you, do not worry about your life, what you will eat; nor about the body, what you will put on. Life is more than food, and the body is more than clothing. Consider the ravens, for they neither sow nor reap, which have neither storehouse nor barn; and God feeds them. Of how much more value are you than the birds? And which of you by worrying can add one cubit to his stature? If you then are not able to do the least, why are you anxious for the rest? Consider the lilies, how they grow: they neither toil nor spin; and yet I say to you, even Solomon in all his glory was not arrayed like one of these. If then God so clothes the grass, which today is in the field and tomorrow is thrown into the oven, how much more will He clothe you, O you of little faith? And do not seek what you should eat or what you should drink, nor have an anxious mind. For all these things the nations of the world seek after, and your Father knows that you need these things. But seek the kingdom of God, and all these things shall be added to you. Do not fear, little flock, for it is your Father's good pleasure to give you the kingdom. Sell what you have and give alms; provide yourselves money bags which do not grow old, a treasure in the heavens that does not fail, where no thief approaches nor moth destroys. For where your treasure is, there your heart will be also" (Luke 12:22–34; NKJV).

There is no question where my father's heart was focused or where his treasure was to be found. He, like the Apostle Paul, showed through his life choices that he considered "all things loss for the excellence of the knowledge of Christ Jesus my Lord, for whom I have suffered the loss of all things, and count them as rubbish, that I may gain Christ" (Philippians 3:8; NKJV).

Over the years and through times of extreme pain and sorrow, my mind has traveled back over the years to visit these golden days of my earliest memories. Although I cannot recall my mother or father actually instilling within us the meaning behind Paul's words in Philippians 4:8, I saw them live a life before me that embodied Paul's message: "whatever things are true, whatever things are noble, whatever things are just, whatever things are pure, whatever things are lovely, whatever things are of good report, if there is any virtue and if there is anything praiseworthy—meditate on these things." It is not the lack of niceties that I recall, it is the joy in the few luxuries we had. It is not the crushing weight of the communist system that is ingrained in my early memories; it is the freedom we enjoyed to love one another in a godly household. I don't recall living in cramped poverty; I remember golden days that stretched out before me like a playground of dreams.

Life Lesson 1: Focus on Hope

The USSR during the days of my youth was a veritable hotbed of atheistic, manipulative tactics designed to replace human ingenuity and faith with socialistic conformity. Christianity was diametrically opposed to all communistic agendas and my family was distinctly and unapologetically Christian. Outspoken Christians were watched and any deviation from accepted communist doctrine could bring swift and harsh consequences. Christians in the USSR were hounded, maligned, and often faced imprisonment or were committed to insane asylums. My parents faced these threats daily, yet never wavered in their faith or its expression. They did not give lip service to serving God, nor did they fail to live their faith. I watched them daily take up the cross (Luke 9:23) with joy in their hearts and hope leading them ever forward, regardless of the obstacles placed in their way.

Had my parents focused on the circumstances of their earthly lives, I can only imagine the destructive affect it would have had on their outlook. To work endlessly, knowing no amount of work would ever create a better quality of life for them or their family—this alone could have caused them to despair of the will to go on.

My parents chose to focus on the Lord instead of on the world. They focused on His promises rather than the world's threats. They focused on His goodness and refused to dwell on the godless society that surrounded them. They taught me by example to focus on the truth; they trained my eyes to see the noble, just, pure, lovely things around me. They spoke about the goodness of God, extolling His nature and singing His praise. They taught me to "think on these things." For in this is the way of hope; and "hope does not disappoint, because the love of God has been poured out in our hearts by the Holy Spirit who was given to us" (Romans 5:5).

Consider this:
1. What things in your life serve to cause your eyes to stray from the goodness of the Lord to the circumstances surrounding you?
2. What do you believe Paul means when he says, "meditate on" the truth?
3. What do you believe Paul means when he says, "meditate on" the noble, just, pure, lovely things that surround you? What are those things in your life?
4. How do you believe meditating on God's goodness and singing His praises can affect your outlook on life?
5. What circumstances in your life tempt you toward negative feelings and outlooks?
6. How can focusing on the negative bring hopelessness into your life?
7. How can focusing on the positive bring hope into your life?
8. What steps can you take to train your mind to think on the things that will bring hope?

Chapter Two

Broken Hope

My parents were wise; they allowed their children the freedom to choose to follow the Lord without any pressure from them. So in December of 1976, when mom encouraged me to attend an upcoming New Year's Eve youth gathering at church, I agreed to go. That night changed

> Proverbs 3:5, 6
> "Trust in the Lord with all your heart, and lean not on your own understanding; in all your ways acknowledge Him, And He shall direct your paths" (NKJV).

my life forever. I opened my heart and wept on my knees in repentance. Peace and joy poured as liquid love into my heart when I repented from all things of the world that had arrested my attention. I dedicated my life to following the path God desired for me. I was no longer the same Galina. I felt a burning love in my heart for my Savior who died for me on Golgotha's cross. I knew my heart had been made new because happiness, joy, and gratitude filled me to overflowing; I was overwhelmed! I determined that I would live my life free from any casual, romantic involvement and would focus my attention on serving the Lord with all the youthful vigor I could muster.

From that time, I surrounded myself with members of the church youth group. While we enjoyed worshiping in the state-sanctioned Baptist church, we wanted more fellowship. We were frustrated with government control and undercover informants; we longed for the freedom to worship the Lord and share our faith. Many members of my youth group and some young married couples began to gather for unsanctioned, home fellowship meetings. It was in these meetings that my faith took wings. Finally, when I was 15 years old, a number of my friends and I left the registered Baptist church altogether and became an "underground church."

Our band of believers met in secret, but operated fearlessly on the streets. We witnessed to anyone who would listen and lived out our faith in any way we could find. Of course, our "traitorous" group became known to the police; sometimes, they would find out where we were meeting and break up our service. One such time was when I attended a large outdoor youth convention in a wooded area. The police encircled our gathering, escorted dozens of us aboard a waiting bus, and took us to the police station. While there, an officer held up a Bible and lectured us: "You young people are the avant-garde of our society. I wish everyone could be like you. If everyone could live by the New Testament, it would be communism. Only there is one problem, we need to do it without God!" Without pause or fear, our group leader stood and said boldly, "We are the way you describe precisely because of our God and His Word. That's why we are conscientious, good workers and citizens." We were finally allowed to leave, though we all knew the persecution would continue. We experienced many such episodes; through them all, our faith only grew stronger.

After a few years in the underground church, on the night of August 28th, 1978, I was baptized in the Kuban River (public baptisms were illegal). I'll never forget walking into the water, dressed in a long white robe. The light of the moon shimmered on the water like a carpet of gold stretched out before me. It was a night of pure joy. I received communion for the first time after I was baptized. Then the pastor prayed for those of us who'd been baptized to receive the Holy Spirit. How sacred, glorious, and holy all of this was to me! I understood deeply that nothing could ever replace my relationship with my God. The words of King David, found in Psalm 62:5 rang in my soul: "Yes, my soul, find rest in God; my hope comes from him." I would not fully realize the power of King David's words until much later in my life. But as much as possible, at that young age of 16, I began to understand nothing and no one in life was greater or more trustworthy than my God. Then, still damp from my proclamation of faith, I walked on air toward my home. Through every step of the two hour walk back, I repeated my promise to God to serve Him with a pure heart and conscious desire. This was my very first covenant with God

After my spiritual awakening and baptism, the rest of my teen years were spent doing all I could do to live out my faith. I came to understand much about the words of James: "faith by itself, if it is not accompanied by action, is dead" (James 2:17; NKJV). My friends from church and I visited the sick and needy of our congregation; we shared our faith by singing Christian songs on the public transportation; we shared the gospel with strangers. It filled me with purpose to share my knowledge and beliefs with those who understood life differently. I felt grateful to be of help to those who were disappointed by life. I was thrilled to be able to share hope, especially with those who, on their deathbeds, feared dying. (How terrible to face death without knowing the Author of life.)

As I neared my twenties, the young men of the congregation began to flirt and shower me with attention. However, according to the standards of my church, young men and women did not date; they didn't hold hands and were never to be alone together. All contact was to be in groups or in the presence of parents or leaders. Arranged marriages were no longer the norm; but in my church, there was still close involvement by parents. When a young man decided upon a young woman as his future wife, he would first ask her if she wanted to marry. If she agreed, the next step was the Russian tradition called *Svatovstvo*, which means the young man's parents accompanied him to his future bride's home and asked for her hand and her parents' blessings on their union. If the young woman's parents agreed to the match, the couple could then be officially engaged.

When I was about 16, I noticed a handsome and winsome young man named Yuri. He was a musician and the director of the choir of our underground church. He was everything I desired in a husband and I developed quite a crush on him. Shortly after this, Yuri was conscripted into his mandatory 2-year tour of duty in the army. While he was away, we carried on a pen pal relationship. I was 18 when Yuri was discharged from military service. By this time, I was deeply in love with this young man. I spent long hours alone in my room daydreaming of what it would be like to be his wife. I loved him deeply and tenderly. I lived off the hope that he would, one day, choose me. I begged God to show me a sign that Yuri and I were meant for each other.

One night following choir practice, Yuri asked if he could speak with me. So excited I could barely contain myself, I followed him outside. At first we walked in silence. He was nervous and it took him several attempts to put his words together. Finally, he took a deep breath and looked in my eyes. He spoke very softly, "Galina, I would like to ask you to be my wife." I was completely over-whelmed; it was like champagne flowed in my veins, effervescing through my heart and mind. Instant visions of what life would be like as Yuri's wife filled my consciousness.

I asked Yuri if he had sought God's will before asking me. He assured me that he was certain our marriage was God's plan. I told him I needed to pray about my answer.

Upon my return home, I cried from sheer happiness. I rejoiced on my knees and glorified God that He had answered my prayer and that He had created this miracle for me. I had never known such utter and complete joy. I just knew marriage to Yuri was exactly the right path and determined to tell him so at our next meeting. I absolutely could not wait for that next time together!

The long-awaited day finally arrived and I told Yuri that I'd most certainly be his wife. He replied that we'd be married in a year. His father was away on business abroad and his younger brother was still in the military. Both were expected to return within months. When his brother and father rejoined the family, we would become officially engaged. He asked that I keep our un-official engagement a secret until it could be publically announced. I agreed.

But how could I keep secret such a delicious turn of events? How could I keep quiet when my heart was about to burst with joy that multiplied by the second? I told my best friend and my parents; soon, my entire family knew the reason for my exaggerated joy. The news of my unofficial engagement spread quickly. Trying to keep our love a secret was like trying to hold rain water in my hands; it simply poured through.

Everything in my life was moving along so smoothly and sweetly! I was young and happy and sure that nothing or no one could get in the way of me and my Yuri being together for the rest of our lives.

We saw each other often at church and youth group. Our time together and our phone calls were filled with delight and expectation. Each farewell was a moment of grief, as though we each were forced to abandon a part of ourselves. Our church taught us to avoid all physical affection (even holding hands) in order to guard against physical temptation. Both of us adhered to that standard. It was only in our minds that we expressed any kind of physical affection toward each other. It was the yearning and longing between us that made our phone conversations so treasured.

I floated through my days, lifted high by the lightness of my heart and the buoyancy of my dreams. Even after all the years that have passed since those glowing days, I remember all the details of our conversations and time together like only hours have gone by. But my sublime joy was not to last.

Yuri's father returned home from his business ventures. Days went by and turned to weeks; yet, Yuri's parents did not arrive to arrange with my parents for the official engagement and marriage. Then Yuri began to avoid encounters with me. My feminine intuition felt something had gone awry.

I decided he owed me an explanation. After church one Sunday, I asked him to explain what was going on; what was the reason for him avoiding me? His answer was brief. "I don't know what to do. My parents disapprove of our engagement. I feel like I am between two fires."

Shock reverberated through my heart. My mind could not comprehend what my ears were hearing. My heart longed to see Yuri rise up and stand strong in his right to marry me. I wanted to see him cling tenaciously to our love and our future. I decided to test him, "Now what? Should we break up?" I didn't want to hear those words pass my lips; but I was probing him. I wanted to hear him say he would fight for our love. Instead, I was humiliated and emotionally mutilated when he simply said, "I don't know what to do anymore!"

It was not long after that conversation that Yuri told me his family was adamantly against our marriage. I honestly expected that he would reconsider and pray until his parents changed their minds. But he simply gave up. I told Yuri I would never again trust a Christian man. I asked him, "What will we do now with God's will for us?" He answered icily: "God's will for us is that we go our separate ways." I responded, "How sorrowful it is when we state our own wills and desires as if they are God's."

As I began to process the reality that our marriage would not happen, I began to sink into a desperate depression. I was absolutely certain that we were made for each other. Yuri had assured me our marriage was God's will. How could that fact have changed? My shattered heart could not find peace or solace. We had been so close to finally tasting the joyful fruit of marriage; how could I endure the bitterness of separation and the death of a dream? Each day, the pain increased and even breathing became a torture to my wounded heart. I could no longer feel my legs. My body felt as though it was stuffed with cotton and I could no longer walk. This state continued for days.

My concerned parents called for the doctor. After many probing questions, the doctor assured me that I would find love again. But how could that be possible? How could I ever be whole again? How could I ever trust again? I could not imagine life continuing. I covered my face with the blankets and tried to disappear from life. After some time, I began feeling better. I started getting out of bed and forcing myself to walk.

It was not long before I learned that Yuri was getting married. It happened quickly and made me feel as though the days we spent together meant nothing at all to this man. I spent the day of his wedding with my friends wiping away my tears.

Galina's family when Galina was about 3 years old.
Galina is in Middle standing between her parents

Galina's Father (Alexander) and Mother (Galina)

Portrait of Galina, age 18

Yuri (on right)

Galina with her Grandma Antonina, Yalta 1984

Life Lesson 2: Broken Hope

I have always believed that God gives each of us the right to make our own choices. He gave us feelings and the ability to reason through tough decisions. However, just as He has given each of us free will, He gives every other person in our lives the same freedom to choose. And the decisions we make affect others in our lives; sometimes, our choices can impact people we never see or know.

The end of the Yuri chapter of my life was a monumental turning point. It was the first time in my life that hope had led to hurt in such a deep way. Although I had no control over Yuri's life-changing decision, I did have choices about how I would respond.

Unfortunately, I allowed the trauma to create doubts and questions that cracked the foundation of my faith and corroded my trust in God and Christian men. And so began a silent conflict in my soul, waged in the inner and unspoken language of the spirit. It slowly metastasized until the cancerous-like condition threatened my spiritual well-being and impacted decisions soon to come.

You see, rather than firmly holding to hope in Christ for my future, after my breakup with Yuri, I allowed myself to fall into despair. Because of this, I was an easy target for the fiery darts of the evil one. He planted questions and doubts in my young mind that would cause most of the color and texture of my faith to wash from my life.

Filled with hurt and overcome by rejection, I allowed myself to let my hope waver and permitted my trust in God's faithfulness to grow dim. This is a road that leads to misery. And the road I was on led to untold grief and sorrow.

Consider this:
1. Has there been a time in your life when you held to a hope that ended in sorrow? How so?
2. In what way could imperfect choices or faulty understanding have played a role in the resulting pain?
3. In what ways did you find your faith wavering in the face of the trial?
4. James 1:2–7 says, "My brethren, count it all joy when you fall into various trials, knowing that the testing of your faith produces patience. But let patience have its perfect work, that you may be perfect and complete, lacking nothing. If any of you lacks wisdom, let him ask of God, who gives to all liberally and without reproach, and it will be given to him. But let him ask in faith, with no doubting, for he who doubts is like a wave of the sea driven and tossed by the wind. For let not that man suppose that he will receive anything from the Lord; he is a double-minded man, unstable in all his ways." Obviously, there is a tie between trials and the blessing of wisdom. In your own understanding, what is this tie?
5. How do you believe your own painful circumstance worked to increase your patience and wisdom?

6. Can you see ways in which you were "double-minded" in your reaction to your own trial? What affect did this have on your life?

7. In your own understanding, what is the tie between patience, wisdom, and hope?

Chapter 3

Impossible Hope

After my broken engagement, my life was going nowhere. My dream of being a wife and mother had been destroyed by the very one I loved. My education had also been

> Romans 7:19, 24, 25
> "For the good that I will to do, I do not do; but the evil I will not to do, that I practice . . . O wretched man that I am! Who will deliver me from this body of death? I thank God—through Jesus Christ our Lord" (NKJV).

cut short. During the time of my engagement to Yuri I was in college studying seamstress technology which would have qualified me for a career in the factory production of clothing, eventually including supervision and management responsibilities. After I turned eighteen, the program director strongly encouraged me to join the communist party. But because of its requirement to promote atheistic propaganda, I refused. The director told me that party membership was necessary to advance my career and because I wouldn't join I was finally asked to leave the program. By the time Yuri and I broke up I was a well-trained seamstress, but I only had a high school diploma. I felt choked by the brokenness of my life. I didn't want to stay in the city where all my memories of Yuri were still so alive; even though it had been almost two years since our breakup, I just couldn't stand to be in Krasnodar any longer.

So in 1983, I moved to the seaside city of Yalta, about 300 miles west of Krasnodar—a full day's journey from my home and family. While a bit intimidating, a change of scenery and new experiences beckoned me as a balm for my pain. I soon fell in love with this paradise on the shores of the Black Sea. I was captivated with its crashing waves, the smell of salt water and seaweed, the call of the swooping and diving seagulls, and the silhouettes of the mountains in the background. On my own for the first time in my little one-bedroom apartment, I was twenty-one and filled with hopeful thoughts of new adventures and possibilities.

I started attending services at the Yalta Baptist Church; but the pain and disappointment that enveloped me after the collapse of my supposedly godly relationship with Yuri had hardened my heart. I doubted all I had been taught about godly relationships. Rather than recalling the love between my parents or looking to other good marriages as an example, I chose to question whether limiting my relationships to only Christians was really important after all. My jaded eyes told me that Christian men were no better than non-Christian men and it didn't really matter which one I married.

My first week in Yalta was spent looking for work. I began by checking on companies who employed seamstresses, but no jobs were available. As I strolled the boardwalk, wondering what to do next, I noticed a number of professional photographers taking outdoor portraits for tourists. I spoke with one of them and found out the name and address of their company. I had enjoyed photography as a hobby and decided to apply for a position. To my pleasant surprise, I landed a position right away as an apprentice photographer and absolutely loved my job. Most often, I too was assigned to the seaside boardwalk and offered my services to the tourists vacationing in Yalta. What a gorgeous, light-hearted place it was! Numerous people roamed up and down the boardwalk; musicians were everywhere; artists set up their easels and drew or painted portraits and landscapes. All along the boardwalk people played and relaxed in the bright, seaside sun. Dolphins played in the surf and children's laughter echoed across the entire scene. I loved taking photos in that beautiful place.

One day, my camera needed repair; I took it to our company repair shop. The repairman, Vasily Losev, seemed interested in me and made his attraction apparent. We talked for quite a while. I must admit, my wounded ego and pride absorbed the attention like a sponge. The next day, I went back to pick up my camera. Vasily's interest seemed to have grown overnight. He invited me to go swimming with him after work. Meeting with young men I didn't know was totally foreign to my experience in life, but I agreed to meet him. We spent the evening together just talking and swimming. After our little date, he offered to accompany me home. I was interested to learn more about him, so I accepted.

We walked a full hour to my apartment so we could have more time to spend together. The time seemed to fly by as Vasily and I shared our life stories with one another. I told him of my breakup with Yuri and the pain of watching my dreams die. It felt good to give voice to the carnage the breakup had left in my heart.

Vasily told me he sometimes wrote poetry and offered to recite some for me. I encouraged him and was impressed with the beauty of his words. That he would share such an intimate part of himself with me warmed my heart and soothed my wounded ego. Looking back, I realize Vasily was a bit older than I and very experienced at courting women. I was mesmerized by this man!

Vasily was married; he and his wife were in the process of divorce. Jealousy and suspicion had destroyed his marriage and he was left frustrated and angry. Vasily became more and more open as he shared his thoughts and attitudes with me. He even recited a poem he had written about the way his marriage had deteriorated and died. I do not recall much of that poem, but I do remember the final lines:

> House on Fire
> Roaring Flames howl and wine
> Two bodies intertwine
>
> Lovers perish, lovers fly
> Like shooting stars they streak on high
>
> I hope their souls find peace
> I hope their souls find rest
> Together forever beyond the stars

With the clarity of hindsight, I recognize the deranged and dangerous thoughts reflected in Vasily's poem. But, at the time, I had no idea that the twisted words were an evil foreshadowing of future events. Rather, I listened to the poem and tried with all my youthful wisdom to turn Vasily's focus toward reconciliation with his wife and restoration of his marriage. I witnessed to him about the Lord's love and healing power. I explained to him that such thoughts of death and retribution were directly from satan. I encouraged him to open himself to the Lord's love and receive the peace only God could give. I told him that God could and would take care of his problems if he had faith and accepted Jesus as his personal Lord and Savior.

Vasily seemed to listen intently and to accept with interest my attempts to point him toward the Lord. He told me he believed in God and that he and his parents were from the Orthodox Church. Vasily told me he had never before heard anyone talk about having a personal relationship with Jesus and expressed the desire to know more.

When we got to my apartment building, we sat down on a wooden bench under a balcony. It was a beautiful night and my heart was captivated by such a romantic scene. I had never been alone with a young man before in such a potentially compromising situation. It was exciting and there was an element of the forbidden just sitting there with him under the stars.

As we talked, Vasily moved closer and gently placed his arm around my shoulders. He used his gift with words to tell me how impressed he was with my virtues, values, beliefs, and beauty. I suddenly realized I was playing with fire. My heart started pounding and an inner voice told me to end the encounter. Part of me wanted to leave immediately; another part was captured by the magic of his affections. I listened to the latter voice and chose to remain under his spell.

Vasily slowly began to kiss me. He grew more passionate and then became aggressive. The magic feeling evaporated and panic took hold! I tried in vain to disengage myself from his steely grasp. I cried and pleaded with him to let go of me. All my protests just seemed to spur him on. My lips began to feel bruised and swollen. My heart thudded in my chest, I felt lightheaded and dizzy, and nausea threatened to overwhelm me. Hoping to shock him into self-control, I told Vasily I would kill myself should he steal my innocence.

It was then that I heard my conscience speaking to my heart: I should never have allowed this situation to occur. I knew it was absolutely wrong for me to be alone at night with any young man, especially one I had only just met. Conviction erupted within my soul.

Then just as suddenly as it began, Vasily's attack ended. It seemed some animalistic urge within him simply ceased. He begged me to forgive him for such a loss of control. He saw how weak and shaken I was; he swore that if I would allow him to simply walk me to my apartment, he would not touch me again. Feeling as if all strength had drained from my body, I shakily agreed.

He helped me to my apartment and I asked him to leave. Vasily took a few steps toward the door, then turned and came back across the room. The scene on the park bench was nothing compared to the assault he then waged against me. He was determined that he would sleep with me that night and take my innocence with him when he left my little apartment. He tried cajoling and pleading and then physical force. Through fear-filled tears, I fought him with all I had within me. My entire being reeled with terror and shame. Having neared the end of my feeble strength, I repeated that I would kill myself if he succeeded in his fevered purpose. Those words seemed to arrest his attention enough for him to regain control. With a contrite look, Vasily asked forgiveness for breaking his promise. Then he turned, walked out the door and I heard the lock click as the door shut quietly behind him.

I tossed and turned throughout that long, dark night. A grinding pain in my stomach made me wonder if I had eaten tainted food. My head ached nearly as badly as my heart. I was overcome with exhaustion that no amount of sleep could cure. And my poor, damaged, swollen lips throbbed and pulsed with waves of pain. I simply lay in my bed that night awaiting the sun and praising my God that

He had protected me from such a heinous, sinful act. Finally, I fell into an exhausted, fitful sleep.

When the sun rose, I awoke and thanked God that He had protected me from a worse conclusion to the events of the night before. I stared at my reflection in the mirror as the horrifying scenes began to replay through my mind. My dark red, bruised lips were proof of the attack. Shock and shame vied for prominence in my heart as my mind struggled to accept the truth. I had nearly been raped!

No matter what had occurred the night before, I had to prepare for work. I had nearly finished getting ready to leave when the doorbell rang. Still anxious from the night before I walked fearfully to the door thinking maybe Vasily had returned, but instead I found a blessed and timely surprise. There stood two old friends from Krasnodar, Anatoly and his wife Emma with their five year old son Joseph. Anatoly and Emma were devout Christians who had previously operated a station of an underground printing enterprise in the basement of their home. They did the final assembly of a Christian magazine that often included testimonies of persecuted Christians. Eventually the KGB came to know about it and began surveillance of their home. Anatoly was finally arrested and imprisoned for three years. It hadn't been long since his release. It was as if the Lord had sent these strong, Christian friends to uplift and support me in the aftermath of the attack.

I was so overjoyed to see them! It was impossible for them to fail to notice my swollen, bruised lips. When they questioned me, I told them openly, sparing no details about the night before. Just speaking of the attack aloud brought renewed waves of stomach pain and dizziness. With great concern, Anatoly advised me to leave Yalta immediately and go back home to Krasnodar. He insisted that it was not safe for a young woman to be living alone. I reassured him that I had learned my lesson and that I would never allow this to happen again. I simply was not one to give up in the face of trouble and I wanted to stay.

We thanked the Lord for granting us our safety and for giving us His help and protection. Then we all left my apartment and traveled together to the boardwalk where my work day would begin.

I was happy and thankful that my friends were able to sit a while with me as I worked. We continued to catch up and rejoice in our reunion.

Sometime later, I glanced up from my work and gasped. I could not believe my eyes! To my horror, Vasily was walking down the boardwalk toward me. In his hand he held a bouquet of beautiful carnations. He boldly approached and asked if he could have a private word with me. With shocked venom in my voice, I replied, "Leave me alone. I don't need you or your flowers." Vasily was insistent, begging repeatedly for me to forgive him. He expressed shock and horror at his own behavior. But I would not yield. Seeing my unwillingness to accept his flowers, he turned around and threw them into a trash can. He disappeared as quickly as he had appeared.

Anatoly and Emma continued to express their concern for me and to encourage me to leave Yalta behind and return home. But I was resolute in my decision to stay put. Finally, several days later my friends' visit drew to a close and I was left alone once again in my little studio apartment.

Sitting alone that night, I examined the feelings and thoughts that came pouring through my soul. It seemed the passionate instincts Vasily had aroused had awoken the woman within me. I wanted to be loved and desired; I wanted to love a man; I wanted a husband, a home of my own and children. Having had all these things offered and then lost only made them that much more precious to my empty, hurting heart. I thought of Vasily and the fire in his passionate kisses; surely such passion came from true caring. Though it was terrifying, I found myself thinking that, on some level, being so desired felt really good. I immediately tried to block these thoughts from my mind.

Over the next days, I tried to avoid any contact with Vasily. I went to work, attended church, and continued living my life as I had before the incident. But, inevitably, our paths continued to cross at the photo studio where we both worked. Whenever I was within speaking distance, Vasily repeated his claims of sorrow and shame over his actions toward me. He seemed so contrite; after several weeks, I began to soften toward him. My desire for affection overwhelmed my good sense. I could hear God telling me that Vasily was absolutely not for me. Yet, the attention Vasily showered on me was like a magnet, drawing me to him even though I knew it was wrong.

I listened to the voice of my emotions that craved affection and attention. I wanted to be in love with someone. I started to think that Vasily could come to our church and become a Christian. It never occurred to me that Vasily's loss of control was only a warning of worse things to come. I played with fire for the thrill and the excitement and, somehow, I imagined I would not get burned.

What I didn't realize was that satan had already crafted a plan, though well-masqueraded, to catch me in his trap. Satan's plans are always to kill, to steal, and to destroy. Because I refused at this critical time to listen to the voice of God's Spirit within, the trap was laid and the course of my future was set upon a road that led through untold misery and pain. Such is the course satan desires for us all.

Life Lesson 3 – Impossible Hope

Looking back over these events, I am struck by the fact that one decision, one exception to following the guidance of the Lord, resulted in a series of faulty choices. I willingly met with a young, handsome stranger in a way that rejected all I had been taught about proper restraint and modesty between unmarried couples. I knowingly opened my life to someone whose entire life was based on a worldview that was vastly divergent from my own. I chose to make myself vulnerable to a man who did not know the Lord.

How often do we allow ourselves one moment of weakness, thinking no true harm will come? How often do we disregard the still, small voice of our Lord as He gently guides us toward life-giving, life-affirming choices? How often do we justify compromise as a harmless option? How often do we sacrifice future good for present solace?

Though our loving, faithful Lord's forgiveness is always available, each step we take away from Him leads us further down a path of rebellion and compromise. With each sinful choice, we become more and more insensitive to the Spirit's voice within. The Spirit of God may remind us of the truth we've learned; but in the end, we must choose to act on that truth if we are to remain on the path of blessing. Each choice of our lives must be based on the truth of God, not on the desire that clouds our judgment and confuses our minds.

The Apostle Paul put it this way, "For the good that I will to do, I do not do; but the evil I will not to do, that I practice ... O wretched man that I am! Who will deliver me from this body of death? I thank God—through Jesus Christ our Lord" (Romans 7:19, 24, 25; NKJV).

We must depend on our Lord for every moment of life and every step along the way. We are faulty beings whose natural tendencies will always lead to sin. And sin will always lead to sorrow and pain. But Jesus has promised He will never leave us or forsake us (Hebrews 13:5). On that, we can always depend.

Consider This:
1. In looking back over your life, what are times you recall when you've made choices based on the desires of your flesh rather than being led by the Spirit within?
2. What were the results of these choices?
3. Why do you believe you chose to disregard the Spirit's leading?
4. In what ways has the Lord Jesus proven His faithfulness to you following your sinful choices?
5. What choices do you now face in which you are tempted to take your own path rather than the one the Lord desires?
6. Are you attempting to justify these sinful choices? If so, in what way?
7. Take time to listen to the Lord and determine the course He would have you follow. Write your understanding of His leading here.

Chapter 4

Hopeless Heart

The days in the sunny, seaside town of Yalta carried on. I enjoyed my work as a photographer and found the dreamy, vacation atmosphere much to my liking.

> **Hebrews 3:15**
> "Today, if you will hear His voice, do not harden your hearts as in the rebellion" (NKJV).

The problem with living in such a dream-laden atmosphere is that reality soon seems much less attractive. My own reality was vastly different from the merry existence I had hoped to have at this stage of my life. I had set my heart on love and marriage and children, only to have those dreams turn to a nightmare of loneliness and separation from all I had ever known. Happiness seemed a thing of the past and my shallow smiles at new friends and customers never reached my eyes … or my heart. I felt like a dark cloud floating through a sun-drenched sky—out of place and still haunted by the loss of Yuri.

I craved attention and connection to others; Vasily was all too willing to meet me at my point of need. He continued to shower me with praise whenever he happened to see me. He expressed utter disbelief that such a perfect creature as I could exist in the world. To my affection-starved soul, his words were like a lifeline; unfortunately, it was a lifeline that would soon begin to totally undermine the true life I had found in Jesus Christ.

Vasily was in the final stages of a divorce; his second from the same woman. He claimed his pregnant wife had been unfaithful and he wasn't at all sure the child was his. He seemed so sincere and quite appealing in his candid confessions of loneliness and need. I felt totally incapable of turning a deaf ear to this seemingly sensitive, hurting man.

He often shared his poetry; the beautiful, lofty words touched my heart. His words drew me in and I believed I saw within him a loving, hurting, romantic soul, a person who was in much the same place emotionally as I was. It seemed, that aside from God, Vasily could see my wounded heart and grasp the extent of my anguish. I began to fall ... slowly at first as my spirit fought against what my mind and heart embraced.

During these early days with Vasily, I told my parents of our relationship. My father was concerned, disappointed, and hurt that I had betrayed his trust by getting involved with a non-Christian, married man. He made a special trip to Yalta to speak with Vasily. In no uncertain terms, he demanded that Vasily promise to stay away from me and return to his own wife. In response, Vasily and I continued to see each other and I stopped talking to my parents about it.

I had long since stopped walking closely with the Lord, but I still attended church services. Vasily even began to attend services with me. He seemed sincere in his affection and desire to please me. I was blinded by what I wanted to see; and I wiped from my mind the things I preferred to forget. Vasily was like a magnet—he drew my mind and my heart. He was older (by eight years) and so much wiser in the things of the world. I admired him.

Soon after he began attending church services with me, Vasily confessed his love for me. He claimed he thought about me constantly. His words were like bread to the starving—I greedily consumed the sustenance they offered. Rather than recall Vasily's forceful attempt to have his way with me on our first date, I listened to his impassioned claims of penitence. I was flattered that he had found me appealing and grateful that he had not followed through with his violent intent. I somehow saw the fact that he had not taken advantage of me as a positive and chose to force from my mind what could have happened. We dated; we kissed; we held one another close. He awakened feelings in me I felt helpless to resist. What began slowly ended up in a headlong, downward spiral into a blind, obsessive kind of love. I fell in love with the tender, poetic soul I imagined I saw within the man. I agreed to marry Vasily as soon as his divorce was final.

Vasily continually voiced his frustration about remaining with his wife until the marriage was legally dissolved. His unhappiness seemed so deep and overwhelming. My heart hurt for him. By the end of August, only three months after we had met, I agreed to let him move in with me while we awaited his divorce. I told him there would be no intimacies between us until after we were married; I was naïve enough to believe we could keep to this standard. This is only proof of how far from godly reasoning my mind had retreated. This is not what I had wanted: I had wanted to do things right—God's way. But in the wake of hurt and held by the power of earthly passion, I made choice after choice that took me further and further away from God.

Shortly after Vasily moved in with me, the Lord provided a shining opportunity for me to deny my flesh and turn again to His plan for my life.

My father had a childhood friend named Vanya. Over the years I was growing up, our two families had become close. My father spoke to his friend about my situation and again my father came to warn me, this time with Vanya. He even pled with me, against pursuing my relationship with Vasily. But the pain and disillusionment of Yuri's broken promises were still fresh wounds in my soul. I doubted the wisdom of trusting any Christian man. I was completely unsure whether I could even trust myself; I didn't believe I could discern God's will for me. I had tried to follow as closely as I knew how, only to find myself rejected and alone. In the end, I decided Vasily was just as good a choice as any other; maybe even a better choice than a Christian man. Instead of waiting upon the Lord, I decided to take control of my own future and do the exact opposite of Proverbs 3:5; I decided to lean on my own understanding. Again I rejected the council of my father and remained steadfast in my choice to stay with Vasily.

One of Vanya's sons, Paul, had been a good friend during my teen years, even though he was four years younger than I. Not long after Vasily moved into my apartment, Paul called me. With Vasily standing nearby, Paul begged me to exchange letters with him. It was obvious from his tone that he wanted to pursue a relationship. I told him about Vasily and explained that any correspondence between us would simply be a waste of time. As the conversation progressed, Vasily became more and more upset and anxious. Not recognizing jealousy in action, I considered it a compliment that Vasily was so protective of our relationship. The call with Paul ended with me refusing further contact. I was deeply in love with Vasily. We had become lovers and I fully believed there was no turning back.

Still the warnings continued, and looking back I can only conclude that the Holy Spirit was inspiring the harbingers that brought them. Friends from Krasnodar came to visit me and tried to get through the wall I had built around my heart and mind. The youth group from the Yalta Baptist Church arrived one day. I ignored their knock and pretended to not be home. They prayed compassionately for me as they stood in the hall in front of my door. Paul's sister wrote me a letter in which she spoke prophetically that I was inviting disaster into my life. She told me my poor choices would lead to tragedy. I would listen to no one. My heart was hardened toward God and His church; regrettably, I didn't even realize I had developed a heart of stone.

In April of 1984, Vasily's divorce was finalized and I announced to my parents and to the church that I would be marrying Vasily. My father was adamant that I was making a serious mistake. Neither Vasily nor I paid any attention to my daddy. (I still wonder to this day how I had lost track of my respect for him by refusing to follow his advice.) The members of my church tried desperately to help me see the danger I was inviting into my life. Their concern only served to make me angry and consider them unkind and judgmental.

On May 5, 1984, Vasily and I were married; I was already four months pregnant with my first son. I told myself I would continue serving the Lord and living my faith and soon Vasily would become Christian. Yet, I didn't even attend church for four years. I was stubborn; they didn't agree with my choice to marry Vasily, so I turned from them. I was sure I knew better what was right for me. I believed every one of Vasily's words. I believed he would make my heart's dreams come true—to love and be loved, to raise children, and to spend the rest of my life with the love of my life.

We looked forward eagerly to our child. We planned and dreamed of what life would be like as parents. How glorious to anticipate our home being filled with laughter, childish giggles, and the purest of all loves.

When it was my time to give birth to my first son, Vasily frantically rushed me to the hospital and returned home. (In Russia at that time, husbands did not stay with wives in labor.) Vasily was ecstatic; he couldn't wait to welcome his little Dennis. After 16 hours in labor, still the baby did not come. The doctor explained that my baby's face had become wedged at the opening of my cervix. I was warned that if my baby did not move into a proper birthing position, they would need to terminate his life and surgically remove him. I was terrified and suffering incredible exhaustion. Finally, with the help of the doctor's strong hands, my baby was literally pushed from my body. Despite all of the agonizing horror of childbirth, my tiny baby's frail cry filled me with joy beyond any I had ever known.

As a result of the brutal way my baby was pushed from my body, I was in a great deal of physical pain. But the pain in my body took second place to the pain of having empty arms. I wanted my baby! I was told he was too weak to breastfeed. It was two days before I was allowed to feed him. He was so beautiful with his dark eyebrows in perfect arcs, straight nose, and bow lips; too perfect to be real. (Vasily said our little Dennis looked like me.) Only a small bruise on his forehead hinted at the trauma of his birth. I only got to feed him a few times before being told that my little boy had respiratory problems and would need to be bottle fed for some time.

Finally, the doctor told me my son's condition required that he be transferred to a children's hospital two hours away from Yalta. He said my son's lungs were blackened and extremely weak.

The diseased state of his lungs meant Dennis could easily contract pneumonia. Dennis and I were rushed to the children's hospital by ambulance; Vasily arrived soon after by taxi. We were beside ourselves with fear and anxiety. Vasily paced; I prayed. Our little son was admitted to the Newborn Intensive Care Unit.

The next day, my heart drew me to the NICU to see my son. How I longed to hold him! I looked down at that tiny, frail little body lying helplessly in the incubator and my heart broke from longing. Then suddenly, right in front of me, he began to struggle for each breath. I watched him turn blue. I saw him suffocating, his little lungs struggling for air. In a panic, I called the nurses. They sent me back to my room and whisked my son away to be set up on a respirator. My fear was so overwhelming, even tears would not come.

All that sleepless night, the doctors and nurses battled for my son's life. It seemed all life had imploded to a pinpoint that focused on that precious little baby.

Early the next morning, I made my way to the NICU; though I searched frantically, Dennis was not there. Finally, I asked the doctor in charge, "Where is my son?" She asked me to step into her office so she could explain everything to me. An electrifying jolt passed though me; I knew something was terribly wrong!

When we reached the doctor's office, she told me in a soft voice that my son was gone. Despite the doctors' many efforts, my son had not made it through the night. In one instant, all breath was stolen from my body. My mind rebelled and my heart shattered. I wept inconsolably. I could not, would not be comforted. Shock and alarm battled in my mind. How could he be gone? He was only twelve days old! My soul cried out to my little son, my first and only, my darling boy, "How could I have let this happen to your sweet little life?! Forgive me, my little son. How will I ever live on without you?"

Before I could know the joys of motherhood, grief and mourning filled my heart. Questions begged answers: "God, why did this happen? Why did you take my firstborn son? What did I do to deserve this?" I could not seem to fully grasp that my son was gone. How could life possibly continue? I felt like King David, who cried out to God when he lost the baby boy born to Bathsheba. I thought God was punishing me.

All I could do was leave the hospital and return home ... alone. I had to deliver the black news to my husband. The baby we had looked forward to raising, teaching, caring for, and loving; all of this vanished like autumn leaves washed away by rain. Death had taken our son and there was nothing we could do. I pleaded, "Dear God, please give me the courage and strength to get through this and not lose my mind." I sat with Vasily in our apartment near the little-corner we had prepared for our precious Dennis as I broke the news to my husband. We cried and mourned for days. Vasily carved a headstone for Dennis and made his coffin. We laid him to rest on top of a hill in the shadow of the Ai Petri Mountains.

The loss of our little one brought Vasily and me closer together. We tried to live each day looking forward with hope to a brighter future with faith in our love. We believed our love could overcome any obstacle. Though we had suffered a massive blow, life moved forward slowly with its joys, sorrows, and surprises.

Grief is a vicious burden to bear. Although by this time I had not attended church for over a year, I used Christian hymns to help me get through my grief. My prayers continually went up to God for mercy, support, forgiveness, and protection. I knew my faith could pull me through. But as for Vasily ... our Dennis was the second child he had buried (he and his first wife had lost an infant daughter). Vasily began to drink. With time his drinking became heavy. Finally, by the time a year or so had passed after Dennis' death, drunkenness became his "normal" state when he was not at work. I had never been around such behavior and I was appalled, frightened, and confused when alcohol became more important to my husband than any other part of life.

The pain inside Vasily was like a demon driving him to destructive choices and as he turned to alcohol for solace our home life became chaotic. I knew the Lord would heal my husband of his demons if only he would repent and turn to Jesus as his Savior. I prayed continually that he would find the Lord and become the man I knew he could be. Inside Vasily was tender and sensitive, and he truly wanted to do right. He was charming and full of life; without alcohol, Vasily was a wonderful husband. But the days without alcohol became fewer and fewer.

Life went on through endless days of struggling. Then one day, a telegram arrived. My father was suffering from an acute case of pneumonia. He was extremely ill, but refused to go to the hospital. I caught the first flight to Krasnodar to be by his side.

When I arrived, the man I saw bore little resemblance to the father of my childhood. It was obvious upon entering his apartment that my father was in a desperate situation. His breathing was shallow and heavy. His chest rattled and wheezed with each breath. His cough was deep and frightening; it left him weak and completely exhausted after every attack. I tried to convince him to allow us to take him to the hospital. But, in a breathless, stubborn voice, he refused. I stayed with my father for three days; then I had to return to Yalta.

A few days later, on February 18, 1986, my sister, Nadia, and my mother planned to attend the funeral of Nadia's father-in-law. When my father awoke that morning, it was clear his condition had deteriorated during the night. He was rushed by ambulance to the hospital where he was immediately admitted to the intensive care unit. Since no one was allowed to visit intensive care patients, my mother and sister hurried off to attend the funeral. Unfortunately, the hospital was unaware of my father's severe allergy to penicillin. So an IV of the antibiotic was administered without delay. My mom and Nadia were gone only a few hours. They hurried back to the hospital to check on my father. When they arrived, they were told with cold indifference that my father had died. No preamble, no compassion, just hard, cruel reality. My father was gone.

In stunned disbelief, Vasily and I flew to Krasnodar for his funeral. During the flight, I recalled this man who had been the center of our family and the foundation of our home. I remembered his kindness and humor. I ached in the realization that I would never again hear his voice or feel his embrace. His example of simple, strong, and sincere faith was displayed for me as scene after scene played itself out in my mind: my father praying; my father standing strong for his faith in the face of atheistic authority; my father reading God's Word and helping each of his children understand its truths. How could I live without this rock of a man in my life? How could I go on without my Daddy?

The funeral passed in a blur of tears and heartache and it was time to return home. How empty the apartment seemed when Vasily and I walked through our door. Just knowing my father would never again visit, never again bring little gifts and smile at my childish delight, made my home seem hollow and vacant. It was like some aspect of reality had left this world and taken with it a portion of all substance. How could it be possible that I would never again hear his laughter? It could not be real. I cried inconsolably until I could cry no more.

As the days passed, I recalled my father's favorite hymn, *My Home Above*. I knew the ache of missing him and my little Dennis would ever be a part of me. But I also knew the sorrow of parting was not the end. I reminded myself that, one day, I will again see my little son and my precious father in a place where sorrow, pain, illness, and death can never enter. As the reality of our future reunion took hold of my heart, the aching pain of grief grew more bearable each day.

Vasily and Galina's wedding – May 5th 1984

Galina with a basket of mushrooms

Vasily with a basket of mushrooms

Vasily at work in His camera repair shop

Life Lesson 4 – Hopeless Heart

Psalm 62:5 says, "Yes, my soul, find rest in God; my hope comes from him" (NIV). Yet, so often we turn to people, situations, events, or imaginings to fill our hearts with hope. When those things prove themselves to be no more substantial than dreams, we turn confused and defeated eyes toward the world around us and wonder why hope has vanished leaving only pain and sorrow in its wake.

One thing and one thing only will provide us a hope that does not disappoint—our loving and wise Savior, Jesus Christ.

Although I knew this truth and walked the hopeful road of salvation for the years of my youth, I allowed the current events of my life to harden my heart. Rather than preserving a heart that remained receptive to God, I allowed pain and disillusionment to create walls of self-protection at the core of my being. In the face of death and heartbreak, I hid my mutilated heart behind the fortress I had built. In some way, I tried to hide even from the face of God. Very simply, I allowed life events to cause me to back away from the very One who could provide the strength I needed to weather the storms. When they struck, I was left struggling to find Him. I was left on my own in a world besieged by satan's hatred. And the descriptors applied to him in Scripture proved exactly right—he is the father of lies (John 8:44) who seeks only to "steal, and to kill, and to destroy" (John 10:10; NKJV).

As shocking as it is, those who belong to the Lord must make the decision to allow satan to mutilate our lives. How scandalous it is to me that, in a very real way, we can actually allow our minds and hearts to drift so far from God that we end up choosing to walk paths that lead toward weakness and confusion.

A hardened heart at the very core of one who has tasted and seen the goodness of the Lord is a frightful thing. We may justify and try to explain away our walled-off state; but, in the end, we are the ones responsible for our choices. God gave us free will. We can engage our wills toward pressing hard after God in the face of trial; or we can choose to engage our wills toward treading paths that lead away from God and toward the malignant ways of sin and rebellion.

Trouble will come; trial will attack every life. When it does, we must choose to trust God. It must be a conscious choice. If we stand in the midst of trial, allow the chaos to fill our minds with turmoil, and simply get carried away in the whirlwind, it should come as no surprise that our lives suffer untold injury. To not make the conscious choice to trust God is to make the opposite choice, even if it is not done with awareness. In the face of life's sorrows, we must set our wills to line up with the will of God.

Consider this:
1. Read Psalm 42:11. In what way(s) do you see the psalmist setting his will to line up with the will of God?
2. Read Philippians 4:8. How does making a conscious choice come into play in following Paul's advice?

3. Have you ever found yourself carried away by the storms of life into areas of hardness or sin? If so, what was the result? If not, what allowed you to avoid this pitfall?

4. Describe the attitude you believe constitutes a hardened heart?

5. What steps can you take in life to avoid developing a hardened heart?

6. How does hoping in God allow you to avoid the schemes of the enemy?

7. We have discussed how hope and trust are intertwined in the life of a Christian. How can trust help you continue following God even in the midst of sorrow and turmoil?

Chapter 5

Hope Reborn

One night in 1986, about two years after Dennis died, Vasily came home from work and brought a coworker. They were both drunk when they arrived; they continued drinking until late that night. Vasily's friend was too drunk to leave, so he decided to spend the night.

> 1 Peter 1:13–15
> Therefore gird up the loins of your mind, be sober, and rest your hope fully upon the grace that is to be brought to you at the revelation of Jesus Christ; as obedient children, not conforming yourselves to the former lusts, as in your ignorance; but as He who called you is holy, you also be holy in all your conduct, because it is written, "Be holy, for I am holy" (NKJV).

Vasily settled his friend on the couch then came into the bedroom. He asked me a pointless question in his drunken stupor and I responded with frustration. We ended up in a senseless argument. Something in Vasily seemed to snap. He rushed toward me in a rage and knocked me to the floor. I was in shock; my mind could not grasp what was happening. I screamed for help, but his co-worker was unconscious. Suddenly, Vasily's hands were around my throat and he was strangling me with all his strength. The look on his face was pure evil—hatred and disgust stared deeply into my eyes. I tried to scream again in hopes of awakening his drinking buddy who slept only a few feet away. But Vasily only increased the vice grip he had on my throat; I could not breathe, let alone cry out. I struggled frantically; shock reverberated through my being. My husband was trying to kill me! I struggled until all the muscles in my body ached. I clawed at his hands and used all my strength to try and push him from me; but he was too strong. I felt a slimy substance in my nose and mouth—foam had formed as my body began to shut down from lack of oxygen. And still he continued choking me, literally squeezing the life from my body. I felt myself fading away; my mind was overtaken by a black fog. I prayed for God to accept my soul and forgive Vasily; he was a sinner and did not know what he was doing. I could feel every beat of my heart and knew each one could be the last. Then suddenly, I felt his death grip let go.

Once Vasily released me, I struggled to take a breath. The slimy foam still filled my nose and mouth and my body was wracked with convulsive hiccoughs. Finally, I was able to draw in a gulp of life-saving air. By the time I was able to resume regular breathing, Vasily had fallen into an unconscious state.

The next morning, I struggled to open my eyes. Finally, through small slits, I saw my image in the mirror. My face and neck were swollen beyond recognition and covered with dark, angry bruises. I quickly decided to tell my co-workers I had suffered a severe allergic reaction. To this day, I ask myself why I chose to hide the truth and lie to protect Vasily. I still cannot say why I did not report him to the police.

Vasily claimed to have no memory of attacking me. He seemed appalled at what he had done while in a drunken rage and he begged me to forgive him. I hoped the sight of me would be shocking enough to cause Vasily to turn in disgust from alcohol. I convinced myself that such a thing would never be repeated. As the bruises faded and life returned to "normal," I allowed myself to forgive Vasily and believe his promises that he would never hurt me again. I was young enough and naïve enough to convince myself he spoke the truth. But something within me had been forever changed.

After this horrific incident, happiness seemed to be only an elusive concept that had nothing to do with reality. I could not reconcile Vasily's vicious behavior with the husband I thought I'd married. I could not imagine how peace and happiness could ever be mine. God had allowed my heart to shatter with my son's final breath, my precious father had been taken from me, and my husband had turned on me in sadistic anger. My exhausted soul and traumatized heart knew only to call out to God. Although my own disastrous choices had taken me down a path that led further and further from Him, I still knew and understood that I could find peace only in the Savior of my soul.

When Vasily was not drunk, he was a wonderful husband. The sober version of Vasily continually proved how much I meant to him. But his drinking only worsened with time. With the drunkenness came the uncontrollable rage. In between bouts of drunkenness (that sometimes lasted for days on end), Vasily continued to be the tender, sensitive man I believed I had married. It was like two men struggled inside him. When he awoke from an alcoholic rage, he claimed to have no memory of his actions. He would dissolve into tears and beg me to forgive him. He always swore it would never happen again. And I believe he meant it; it just was not to be.

On Christmas Day of 1988, two years after we lost my father, my sister, Nadia gave birth to her fifth child. Only a few weeks later, my mother called to tell me Nadia had been admitted to the hospital in serious condition. (It was the same hospital in which my father had died and also the hospital in which Lyubov, another of my sisters, had once worked.) Nadia was extremely anemic, had contracted severe pneumonia, and had developed a blood clot in one of the arteries in her lungs. I caught the first flight out to Krasnodar.

When I arrived, I found Nadia in the intensive care unit. She was allowed no visitors; not even family. I felt inspired by God to ask the doctor in charge of the ICU if he would break the rules and allow me to see my sister. The doctor explained that my sister's condition was critical. He gave her only a one percent chance of survival! Again, my heart felt the jolt of severe shock. The doctor listened as I explained I had lost my father in that hospital only two years before. Because he was not allowed visitors, he died alone. I begged him to allow me to see my sister. He agreed to allow me five minutes if I could come up with sterile clothing: a smock, shoe coverings, and cap for my head. My mind raced, wondering where or how I could get all of that sterilized clothing. I thanked the doctor, and told him I would return in fifteen minutes.

Having so little time, I flew to the laboratory where my sister, Lyubov, used to work. A woman who worked in the lab remembered my sister fondly. I told her of my need. Within five minutes, I was dressed in the prescribed sterile clothing and waiting to be admitted into the intensive care unit. (I was amazed at how the Lord had given me the idea to go to the lab and how my need was met immediately. God is the Lord of every detail of life!) I prayed. I begged God to forgive my sins. I pleaded with Him for mercy. I asked Him for a miracle. I promised to return to Him if He would touch and heal my sister. As I poured my heart out before the Lord, I felt His presence as I never had before. I knew God had heard my promise. I knew He was with me in that room.

As I was led down the corridor to my sister's room, a gurney holding a sheet-covered body passed. I was struck by the finality of death. My heart was impacted by the truth that this person had entered eternity. I nearly staggered with the sudden realization of the enormity of the choice we must make upon this earth. If we are to know eternal life, we must choose Him. (I believe, to this day, that God arranged the timing of that gurney in order to focus my attention on things of His kingdom.)

When I finally saw my sister, I did not recognize her. She was extremely pale (in Russian, it is called "having no face"). She was so emaciated that her bruised-looking skin hung like a sheet upon her bones. She struggled to breathe as she asked me to deliver a letter of her last words to her husband and children. I agreed. Instead of the five minutes the doctor had granted me I was able to spend about an hour with her before the hospital staff forced me to leave. (This extension of time was another little miracle; the rules in the ICU units of Russian hospitals are normally very strictly enforced.) I sobbed brokenly as I said what I feared would be my last goodbye.

I left the hospital and traveled the few miles to my sister's home. I cried and begged God for mercy the entire way. When I walked through the door, I was besieged by questions from a sea of concerned little faces and a desperately-worried man. We gathered together to read the letter Nadia had written her family. I stayed close to my family as long as responsibilities at home would allow, and then made the long trek back to Yalta.

Not long after I returned home, I received astonishing news; Nadia was on the road to recovery! It took some time, but she soon returned home, ready to resume her role as wife and mother! God delivered my sister from death. God had granted our miracle! My heart fairly sung with joy and gratitude. Praise to Him flowed from my lips. Even when I was unfaithful, He proved Himself EVER faithful, EVER compassionate, and EVER loving.

It was like my faith was reborn. I kept the promise I had made to God at Nadia's bedside in the hospital. After four long years of separation, I returned to my church family and Vasily came with me. I was like the prodigal son returning to my Father, and my heart was overwhelmed with joy and new life. One Sunday, I stood before the congregation that had prayed so diligently for me. I confessed my sins and shared with them my sorrow and repentance. We rejoiced together as a family. I had finally returned home.

For a short time, it seemed my life was headed down a new and promising path; Vasily stopped drinking for a time and I was awash with hope for a wonderful future walking together with our loving God.

But alcohol dependence was like a chain that kept Vasily bound to a life of rage and violence. It seemed the more I prayed for Vasily to turn to the Lord instead of alcohol, the more Vasily drank. And the longer he drank, the more violent he became.

One day, Vasily was extremely drunk when he came home from work. He had just gotten paid and was very happy with himself. He walked to where I stood in the kitchen and started pulling money from his pockets and handing it to me saying, "Look! This is all for you!" I looked him straight in the eye and said, "I'd rather have you sober than have your money." Before I could blink, Vasily grabbed a heavy sauce pan from the stove and smashed it forcefully down on my head. The blow was enough to knock me to the floor. I lay there, dazed and confused. When my head cleared, I touched my face and looked at my hand and realized I was bleeding badly.

I cleaned the mess from the floor and washed the blood from my body; but the carnage in my life continued.

Following the death of my little Dennis, I spent five barren years. Looking back now, I believe God was graciously allowing me the opportunity to be free of Vasily and his life-threatening alcoholism, without having children to consider. In fact, our wedding ceremony had been a civil affair only, with no vows before God or the Church. For these reasons I now believe it is possible that our 'marriage' never truly existed in the eyes of God. In the spiritual realm then, I believe it could have been interpreted as fornication rather than marriage and that I would have been free to repent of it and divorce Vasily, especially since he had already nearly killed me. But at the time this perspective was not clear to me. Instead my decisions were based on the situations and my emotions. For example, about eighteen months after Nadia's miraculous recovery, I found out I was pregnant. I was beyond thrilled. I so wanted to love and mother a child. I hoped Vasily would be so overcome with love for this coming child that alcohol would finally be banished from his life. These kinds of circumstances, thoughts and feelings kept me in the relationship, always hoping it would change.

Soon after I discovered we were to have a child, we went on a bus trip to visit Vasily's brother in Sevastopol. The road we traveled wound along the mountainous coast of the Black Sea . Sheer cliffs on one side dropped hundreds of feet to sea level. On the way home, I was napping with my head resting on Vasily's shoulder when a loud noise burst through the bus. The driver shouted, "The brakes have failed!" He did all he could to stop the bus, but we crashed into the guardrail along the sheer rock cliff. The front of the bus hung precariously over the edge. We could feel it leaning but it was like something held it in place. We were shaken and bruised, but everyone was alive! The bus driver bravely maintained his composure; the only sign of nervousness was how rapidly the cigarette clenched in his teeth burned into a dangling finger of ashes and cloud of smoke that hovered around his head. First he ordered everyone to slowly move to the side of the bus away from the cliff. Then, under his steady direction, we exited through emergency windows and the back door. A passing military troop transport also stopped and the soldiers rushed to the bus and helped the passengers safely to the ground. How do I express the gratitude and love of life that washed through me? The birds sang around me, the sea breeze blew my hair and caressed my skin, flowers bloomed in brilliant bushes, perfuming the air with their intoxicating scent. My mind and heart were filled with the powerful strains of *How Great Thou Art.* I was alive and my God had mercy on me, yet again!

I was immersed in this deep appreciation for life throughout my pregnancy. What could be better than the feelings of motherhood? Even the morning sickness did not detract from the glow of pregnancy. I will never forget the feelings of happiness and honor that God would entrust me with this new life.

After my experience with Dennis' birth, I was frightened that my baby would be harmed by natural birth. So I opted to undergo a Caesarian Section. I never again wanted to see the hospital where my first little son had lost his life; so I chose a hospital in Alushta, a town forty minutes from home. On the morning of November 4, 1989, our little Aleksey was born. He was perfect; there were no complications and our little boy was healthy and beautiful. I had finally received my heart's desire—I was a wife and a mother. But rather than the joyous occasion serving to arrest Vasily's use of alcohol as I had hoped, it seemed instead that his addiction escalated daily.

With my marriage being nothing but an endless cycle of alcoholic rage and penitent tears, my little Aleksey became the center of my world. After dreaming of having a child for so many years, my dreams had become reality in the form of a tiny blue bundle. My being fairly vibrated with the intensity of love I felt toward my little son.

One night when Aleksey was tiny, Vasily came home in a particularly vile mood. He'd been drinking even more than normal. I don't even remember what set him off; but he became excessively violent and overtaken by a blind rage. He grabbed little Aleksey and ran to the balcony of our third floor apartment. He looked back at me with evil intent as he held our baby in his arms over the edge of the balcony. My heart stopped! I begged and pleaded with all the strength of my being. But Vasily simply stated he wanted to drop our son, break his back, and watch him die. After about fifteen minutes of abject terror, Vasily cradled Aleksey in his arms and put him into his little bed. Then Vasily calmly climbed into bed and went to sleep. The next morning, I was still traumatized. I asked Vasily how he could do such a despicable thing. Vasily told me he remembered nothing of the night before. He assured me he could never put his son in danger.

In August of that year, my mother and brother, 14-year-old Peter, came for a visit. One evening during their visit, Vasily came home very drunk, very aggressive, and very angry. When I tried to calm him down, he started to push me around. Peter tried to protect me. Vasily became violent. He grabbed a hatchet and began to chase us. I tried to grab Aleksey from his crib, but Vasily caught me, ripping my robe as he jerked me to him. He held the hatchet against the back of my neck, threatening to kill me and Aleksey. Somehow, I got Aleksey and we all escaped. We ran down the staircase; Vasily chased us with the hatchet, screaming in a hideous voice. We made it to a phone and called the police; they took Vasily away. We quickly packed some bags. But Vasily was back before we left. He began to apologize profusely. I didn't want to hear anything from him; I had heard enough. We called a taxi as he begged me to stay; he kept asking what he could do to keep me from leaving. I told him the only thing that could make a difference was for him to repent and give his life to the Lord. Then we left and went to stay at a friend's house for several days.

During the time I was away, I went to see Vasily at work because I needed money. He gave it to me. Then he told me that on the day I left him, he went to the evening worship service and accepted Jesus in his heart. He showed me my Bible and where he had written the date: August 16, 1990.

I did not return to Vasily. Instead, Aleksey and I went to Krasnodar with my mom and brother. After a couple weeks, Vasily came to see us. He told my family that he couldn't live without me and Aleksey. He explained that he had accepted the Lord and become a

Christian. He swore he was a different man. My mom couldn't believe him. But I heard the words I had so longed to hear. I told my mother that we must forgive as Jesus forgives. I packed our things and went back to Yalta, full of hope for a new beginning.

For several weeks, life was wonderful. Vasily and I went to church together and life was peaceful. Much to my surprise, Vasily even helped around the house and volunteered to care for little Aleksey.

Then, one day, Vasily came home drunk and the illusion came to an end. I lost count of how many times over the following months I was forced to take my little son and spend the night with neighbors. I had hoped Vasily's claim of finding the Lord was true. Such was not the case. At one point, I spent two months in my pastor's home out of fear of my husband's violent meltdowns. But following every alcoholic episode, Vasily would find a way to soften my heart and convince me that his behavior appalled himself most of all. He would sober up, swear off alcohol, and become the best version of himself. I would bring our little son back home, my heart filled with fervent hope that the last time would, indeed, be the last time.

The drunk Vasily would threaten me, insult me, and manhandle me. The sober Vasily would be horrified by his hateful actions and beg through tears for forgiveness and another chance. The warring personalities within him became more and more distinct. But I believed the tender, loving Vasily would one day win the battle. So I stayed ... and prayed.

Life Lesson 5 – Hope Reborn

We began this chapter with 1 Peter 1:13–15. Another translation puts it this way: "So roll up your sleeves, put your mind in gear, be totally ready to receive the gift that's coming when Jesus arrives. Don't lazily slip back into those old grooves of evil, doing just what you feel like doing. You didn't know any better then; you do now. As obedient children, let yourselves be pulled into a way of life shaped by God's life, a life energetic and blazing with holiness. God said, 'I am holy; you be holy'" (The Message).

Did you hear that? Roll up your sleeves and put your mind in gear! Nothing mystical or magical about that. This is no lightning bolt from the blue that determines our choices. We alone can say "yes" or "no" to the temptations of life. Oh, how heartbreaking that we so often choose to say "no" to God and "yes" to the wiles of the enemy of our souls.

Yet, we serve a heavenly Father who stands ever ready to run to meet us the moment we turn back to Him. Before our tentative "yes, Father" can pass by our trembling lips, He is there to wrap His loving arms around us and comfort our self-mutilated souls. In this is true hope—the hope that strengthens and enlivens; the hope that stands strong and sure; the hope that lives eternally.

The choices I made in a confused, disillusioned state set a course for my life that veered sharply from the perfect plan God had for me. When I allowed my hope in Him to die, I staggered blindly into a life of misery and pain. Yet God did not abandon me. He never left my side; I am the one who turned from Him. And the moment I turned my eyes back to the lover of my soul, He gathered me into His loving embrace. The pain of past hurts was drowned in the rush of love that poured into my heart. And hope was reborn.

I still ask myself "what if?" What if Vasily had actually humbled himself before the Lord and opened his tortured heart to God's healing touch? What if he had been sincere in his desire to meet his loving heavenly Father? What if he had reached out for the only true hope any heart can find? For that miracle of love to bring peace, one must recognize sin and determine to turn away from it, no matter how difficult the process may be. Vasily was truly sorry for his disastrous choices. But he never truly repented—he never truly turned away from his sin.

Sin will kill all semblance of hope. Sin will isolate you inside your own heart and mind where hope is only illusion. Repentance, on the other hand, is the very soil in which hope can flourish; for the heart of repentance is a humility that recognizes that only in God can our souls find rest.

Consider this:

1. Read Psalm 62:5–8. What does this passage tell you about hope?
2. What steps can you take in your life to put into practice the wisdom of this passage?
3. What ties do you believe exist between a hopeless state and sin?
4. How can hope help you avoid temptation?
5. Is there an area of your life in which you fight to avoid temptation? How so?
6. What wisdom can you glean from 1 Peter 1:13–15 to help you stand strong in the face of temptation?

Chapter 6

Insubstantial Hope

It was 1991 and life in Russia had become nearly impossible. Gorbachev's reformation movement, characterized by glasnost (the process of open government) and perestroika (restructuring of the government) had failed. The Soviet government and societal system were in a state of collapse.

> Matthew 7:24–27
> "Therefore whoever hears these sayings of Mine, and does them, I will liken him to a wise man who built his house on the rock: and the rain descended, the floods came, and the winds blew and beat on that house; and it did not fall, for it was founded on the rock. But everyone who hears these sayings of Mine, and does not do them, will be like a foolish man who built his house on the sand: and the rain descended, the floods came, and the winds blew and beat on that house; and it fell. And great was its fall" (NKJV).

The economy followed suit with the disintegrating government. For Americans it was a Cold War victory, for us it became a struggle to survive. The familiar stability of my homeland became a distant memory as the climate of our country changed with dizzying speed. Lies from the government and the devaluing of the ruble (Soviet currency) ran rampant, leaving disillusionment and poverty in their wake. It had been difficult as a Christian in an atheist society, however at least the economy had been relatively stable during my childhood and young adult years. No one could understand why the government had allowed everything to collapse with no viable alternative to replace it.

Prior to the economic collapse, Vasily and I had started a chicken project, together with his parents, in an effort to earn enough money to buy our own car. They raised the chickens on their small farm in Zernivoya; Vasily and I developed a market for them among restaurants in Yalta. We worked hard for our dream, regularly making the four-hour, one-way trip to do the butchering. Vasily found ways to transport the chickens to customers. However, yet another of my dreams died when hyper-inflation dramatically decreased the value of our profits. As common citizens, the lofty ideas of glasnost and perestroika meant that the 15,000 rubles we saved (at one time, enough to buy a car) was only worth a couple loaves of bread. It meant working for months at a time with no paycheck. It meant going without meals and making long trips to Zernivoya for produce and meat generously provided by Vasily's parents. Many became despondent and turned to alcohol. All of this was happening, in addition to living with my own alcoholic husband. I put my trust in the Lord to make it one day at a time.

Even in the face of economic collapse, we had Alexey to take care of and life had to go on. In the beginning of 1992, I discovered I was pregnant again. With joy and hope overflowing my heart, I praised God for His gracious love. I hoped beyond hope that the blessing of another child would help Vasily find the courage and strength to become the man God wanted him to be.

But still, Vasily was powerless over his alcohol addiction, despite the fact that he desperately wanted to stop drinking. His dependence had grown to the point where he needed alcohol to survive. Embittered by the difficulty of earning a living wage in the midst of the economic collapse, he continued disappearing on his drinking binges, often for days. Sometimes, he would come home filled with rage, making insidious threats. When that happened, I would take little Aleksey and run to my neighbors for refuge. When Vasily sobered up, I would return home and try again to hold my family together.

One evening, when I was five or six months along in my second pregnancy, Vasily came home in a particularly agitated, drunken state. Set off by something inconsequential, he stared at me with hatred through cold, dead eyes. I can still see the sneering, wicked smile on his face as he rushed at me. I can still feel the pain that exploded in my abdomen when he kicked me with incredible force. My legs shook, and I nearly fell. My hands flew to my belly; it felt hard and unyielding and I no longer felt my baby's movements.

Vasily dropped to his knees and began to beg desperately for my forgiveness. But my heart had turned to stone; to me, he looked like a wild animal and I abhorred him. Not even animals would do such a despicable thing to their own child! I wept as though I would never stop. I was overcome by fear that my husband had killed my child. I could not comprehend the evil in this man. I couldn't understand such violence against a totally innocent, unborn child. How could he do this?

The next morning, my abdomen was discolored by a massive bruise. I visited my doctor to find that my baby's heartbeat was still strong, but any lasting effects from the trauma would only be known after the child was born.

Every day for the rest of my pregnancy, I prayed fervently for my little child, begging God for health and wholeness. My gracious God heard my desperate pleas. On September 4, 1992, little Alexander was born completely healthy. He was such a good-looking baby—rosy pink cheeks and big, dark eyes! My recovery was quick. To our joy, Alexander grew very strong, healthy, and smart. I thanked my merciful heavenly Father for hearing and granting my prayers.

With every violent episode, my love for Vasily grew colder and my hope dimmed. I wanted to leave him, but at that point in my life, I firmly believed, no matter *what*, marriage is to be forever. Somewhere deep inside me a little spark of hope for Vasily still lived and I had two sons who needed a father. Beyond those convictions hung the truth that I could not support myself and my sons alone; the economy was dead and life was a battle for survival. Then too, Vasily's name was on the deed to my apartment—the legacy my father had left me—and Vasily had no intention whatsoever to be the one to leave. By 1992, my family members were all in the process of immigrating to the United States and, if I left Vasily, I would have nowhere to go. So I stayed.

The struggle to simply survive in Russia grew to epic proportions. Near the end of 1992, we decided to follow my family's lead and file paperwork to begin the long and tedious process of immigrating to the United States. The idea of moving to America was like a beacon in the darkness that offered the promise of a new start.

As the children grew over the next three years, they seemed no worse for the unstable life that surrounded them. Sadly, having known no other way, Aleksey and Alexander seemed to accept the cycles of their father's drunkenness, our flights to refuge, and Vasily's repentance as normal. Our days continued on their chaotic course.

One summer evening in 1995, when Alexander was about 3 years old, I was sitting on the bed in my room; Vasily stormed in wielding a sharp kitchen knife. That began a nightmare that seemed never-ending. My children watched my husband hold me at knife point throughout the night; he threatened to kill me and cut my dead body into pieces and throw them in the garbage. As happened often in his intoxicated states, he hallucinated. On this night, as at many other times, he believed he was seeing demons who urged him on in his insanity. At some point just before sunrise, I pushed the knife away from my throat; in the process, my hand was slashed by the sharp blade. The sight of the wound seemed to reach through the evil fog that enveloped Vasily's mind. He dropped the knife and tried to stop my bleeding before falling into a deep, coma-like sleep.

The next morning, I went to a psychiatrist for a consultation. I told him of Vasily's attack and asked him what I could do to get psychiatric help for my husband. The doctor explained that my husband's consent was necessary before help could be offered. I asked, "And when is it you can take him? Do you mean to wait until I'm already diced into pieces?!" To my question, the doctor responded "Unfortunately, only then could he be arrested or forcefully committed to a psychiatric center." I told the doctor that I had two young boys. I tried to make him understand how frightened I was that Vasily would hurt or kill us. I also explained that we were waiting for approval of our application to immigrate to America. The doctor suggested a clever strategy. "Give your husband only two choices," he said, "Offer him a choice between going into rehabilitation or signing a notarized document giving you permission to take Aleksey and Alexander and immigrate to the United States without him." The doctor believed that signing this paper would give Vasily a reason to sober up.

I went home feeling like a death sentence was hanging over me; but I followed the psychiatrist's advice. To my complete amazement, Vasily signed the paper, proving just how adverse he was to entering any kind of rehab program. I gave the document to a friend for safe-keeping. Even with this document tucked safely away, I was fearful for myself and my sons. I felt so alone and helpless. Yet I knew that God was my protector. I knelt and cried out to Him; then I rose and faced yet another day.

Only about a month later, the situation with Vasily plummeted to a new low. He had been drinking during the day. Later in the evening, he decided to take 5-year-old Aleksey with him while he continued his drinking spree. I tried to stop him, but failed. I waited anxiously for their return, which happened much sooner than I expected. Vasily was obviously frightened and his shoes were covered with blood when he stormed back into the apartment. Aleksey's little face was ashen and he cried fearfully. In a broken little voice he told me, "I don't ever want to go anywhere with Daddy again!" Between my drunken husband and my terrified child, I managed to piece together what had happened. While waiting to buy a beer at a kiosk, a man had cut in line in front of Vasily. Vasily was already drunk and chaffing for a fight. So, in Vasily's words, he "put the guy in his place." He attacked the man, knocked him down and beat him very badly. Aleksey's description of what Vasily had done to the man while he had him on the pavement was so gory and horrifying it sounded like a certainty he had killed him. Vasily also said that he was most likely dead; and if by some small chance he was still alive he would be completely incapacitated for the rest of his life due to the extent of the head injury he inflicted on the man. But he didn't stay around to find out. Before the police could arrive, he had ran off and returned home to hide. I was appalled! My husband may have killed a man with his bare hands. And our little son had witnessed the entire terrible scene!

Early the next morning, I told Vasily we needed to discover what happened to the man he had beaten. Vasily was livid. He coldly told me that he would beat me in the same way if I ever told a soul what he had done. I feared for my children should I lose my life; so I buried the brutal truth deep in my battered heart. Vasily took off to parts unknown for fear he would be arrested and found guilty.

I could no longer find it in my heart to go on. I could not live with a cold-blooded killer. So I made good use of the time Vasily was away to file for divorce. The divorce proceeded smoothly; neighbors testified to Vasily's drunken violence and Vasily never showed up at any of the hearings. The judge finally waived Vasily's rights to contest and granted me a divorce. All that remained to make it official was to have the documents notarized and filed. I consulted with the pastor of my church before taking this final step. He voiced his support of my decision, as did my close friends. They were all too aware of the danger my sons and I faced daily. My decision was clear. I would soon be free of Vasily and his drunken rage. I planned to have the divorce documents finalized as soon as I could arrange the time.

After Vasily had been gone for two months, the boys and I came home one day to find him, his mother, and his brother in the apartment. The children were starved for the attention of their father and they literally crawled all over him. They jumped on his back, rambled in his lap, mussed up his hair, and wrestled with him on the floor. Vasily's response was sincere; the good, loving, and sober father in him had shown up this time. He planted kisses on both boys and tearfully swore he could not live without them. I was amazed at the strength of the relationship between them even after all that had happened. This was the Vasily I wanted and loved and missed and wished I could have always.

The joy of the moment ended when I told him I had obtained a divorce while he was gone. He was confused and very disappointed. He begged me to take him back and give him one more chance. His brother and mother pleaded. Aleksey and Alexander looked hopefully up at me and added their little voices to the pleas. This scene was powerful and I didn't want to deprive my boys of the joy that I saw between them and their father. So I decided to give Vasily another chance and I did not finalize the divorce. Instead, I obtained a new copy of our marriage license.

For the next eight months, Vasily was a different man. The psychiatrist's advice was working. He acted like the husband of my dreams. He stopped drinking and focused on being the best father and husband he could be. One example was how he made long trips across the city every few days to get fresh goat milk for Alexander, who couldn't tolerate the cow's milk we normally bought. He gave us the best he had to give. Bit-by-bit, I relearned how to smile and enjoy life free from danger, stress, arguments, and scandal. It was like a fairytale had materialized in my home. The nightmare of the past faded from memory as my children and I slept night after night safely and peacefully under our own roof.

Early in 1996, after four long years, the paperwork granting us immigration to the United States was approved. My friend still had the notarized document from Vasily giving his permission for me and our two sons to immigrate to the U.S. without him. The knowledge that I had that document had helped him remain sober for eight months. I waited anxiously to see if Vasily's transformation would again evaporate into thin air.

Then I found out I was expecting our third child. Life seemed blessed beyond all I had ever hoped. Everything was on a new course and happiness filled my heart and our days. I was certain this child I carried would never know the trauma my two boys and I struggled to forget. While peace reigned in our home, Vasily tried to convince me to give him the notarized document as proof I had truly forgiven and trusted him. His pleading became more insistent and desperate as time went by. Finally, thinking the document was no longer valid because I was pregnant with our third son, I gave it to Vasily. That very day, Vasily came home drunk. My eight-month fairytale ended as surely as any dream.

It seemed Vasily had not yet reached the depths of degradation. The person he became was one with no logic, reason, caring, or humanity. He was so far gone in the haze of alcoholism that he no longer cared about anyone or anything else. Again, I lived a life of sorrow and regret. If not for my little boys and the child in my womb, I would have despaired of life.

Just before time to deliver my third child, I went to my doctor for a regular check-up. The doctor claimed he could not find a heartbeat and advised an immediate abortion. I refused to believe his unbearable words. I told the doctor I would be aware if my baby had died and I was certain he was wrong. A friend and I prayed throughout the rest of that day: "Dear God, in you I put my trust. You are my shield and protector. God, protect me and have mercy on me."

The next morning, I visited another doctor who performed an ultrasound. I will never forget the moment when he pointed out the tiny, pulsating heart. My child was not dead! I wept with relief and gratitude that I had not heeded the advice to abort this tiny child. (Afterward, I leaned that the first doctor had lied to me because he thought my pregnancy to be ultra-high risk. I considered his actions despicable. Such situational ethics were not unusual in a godless society.)

The day arrived for my little one to be born. I left for the hospital; Vasily continued drinking. Friends from church had agreed to look in on my boys who would be in their father's care. I asked God to protect them while I was away.

My pregnancy had been difficult. When I entered the hospital for the C-Section, my blood pressure was chronically elevated and my kidney function was greatly limited due to the strain the pregnancy had caused on my body. But the C-Section was performed and my third son came into the world in perfect health.

When the anesthesia wore off, I awoke to find myself swollen like a balloon. My kidneys had nearly shut down and my body was slowly being poisoned. The prognosis was bleak. But, oh how powerful the flow of love. The minute my little son, Peter, was brought to me, my kidneys began to work again. Soon, I was breastfeeding my son while on the road to recovery.

I recuperated quickly in the hospital; Vasily drank with his friends to celebrate the birth of a third son.

Friends picked me and little Peter up from the hospital. The whole trip home, I held my newborn infant in my arms and watched the stunning autumn scenery scroll by. The flaming colors on trees seemed to magnify the glory and power of the Creator. I felt His presence so closely that it filled my heart and I sang, *How Great Thou Art*. I saw God's hand of mercy and care in that moment.

The Vasily who met us at the apartment was a stranger to me; haggard and worn. He had lost a front tooth, making him appear foreign. The house was in complete disarray and seemed to mirror the state of my life. Vasily mumbled drunkenly that he loved me and the boys. With slurred, nearly indistinguishable words, he begged me to forgive him … yet again. Anger, sorrow, and regret drained from my heart. Only compassion and mercy remained. I knew that no matter what, I had to care for everyone. It was my task to continue carrying the cross I had chosen. It was a comfort to know that I had the church, my friends, and my kids with me; somehow, everything would be okay. I was certain that God would never leave me, even though I had left Him for so long. He, like a caring father, had always looked after me and had welcomed me back with open arms. He would see me through the future yet to unfold.

Alexey (right) and Alexander (left), Red Square, Moscow 1995

Family Picture, Fresno California, May 1998

Galina with Alexey, Yalta 1989

Vasily and Galina with Alexey and Alexander, Yalta 1992

Life Lesson 6 – Insubstantial Hope

The words of an old hymn ring with truth as I consider this chapter.

"My hope is built on nothing less than Jesus' blood and righteousness. I dare not trust the sweetest frame, but wholly trust in Jesus' name" (Edward Mote; 1834).

"I dare not trust the sweetest frame." How easy it is to allow pleasant circumstance to cloud the Holy Spirit's nudging. During times of trial, we reach up with desperate hands to receive the salvation of our God. When times go well, how easy it is to forsake our walk with God and to follow our own desires.

So many times the Lord, in His great wisdom and mercy, granted me opportunity to flee from the iron grip of evil that held me and my boys in its steely grasp. With our safety threatened, separation was a very valid option that could have been used to promote real and lasting healing; especially because the situation was often violent. However, separation *must* be carefully and wisely undertaken, with adequate precautions, protections, and counseling; especially when substance abuse and mental health issues exist. (Divorce and remarriage is another issue, one beyond the scope of our discussion.)

In any case, I allowed myself to be double-minded—unstable in my thinking; both in my original decision to take up with Vasily and in the early stages of my marriage when I could have taken decisive steps to promote real change. James 1:5–8 says, "If any of you lacks wisdom, let him ask of God, who gives to all liberally and without reproach, and it will be given to him. But let him ask in faith, with no doubting, for he who doubts is like a wave of the sea driven and tossed by the wind. For let not that man suppose that he will receive anything from the Lord; he is a double-minded man, unstable in all his ways" (NKJV). I repeatedly begged God for the madness to end; but, over and over again, I refused to accept God's deliverance. I held to my dreams as the nightmare continued and allowed my own thoughts to drown out the leading of my Lord.

Looking back, I see clearly how the Lord sought to gain my attention and steer me toward a path of blessing. Yet my own opinions of what was right and good blinded me to the voice of God.

We cannot trust in our own understanding when it is clouded with the complications of poor choices; and we cannot allow our own desires and emotions to determine our course. God is continually speaking to our hearts and urging us to follow His path for our lives, which is always based on His principles and His love for us. He always provides a way of escape (1 Corinthians 10:13), if we stay close to Him He will show us the way.

Consider this:
1. Trauma hits each of our lives. Name a time when severe trauma created chaos in your life. What was your response?
2. When has the Lord asked you to veer from the course of your choosing and venture out into the unknown with Him? What was your response?

3. What negative results have you suffered as a result of choosing your own way rather than God's leading?

4. Do you find yourself desperate to hear from the Lord during difficult times and less apt to seek His leading during peaceful ones? What affect does this have on your life as a whole?

5. What does seeking God's leading only during trial say about your relationship with Him?

6. What does seeking God's leading only during trial say of your understanding of Him?

7. Read 1 Corinthians 10:13. What most impacts you about this verse?

Chapter 7

Hopeful Pathway

Life in Russia during the early nineties was chaos. Soviet society had collapsed; and with no plan or money available to build a new system, panic, and devastation followed. The middle class had become poor

> Proverbs 3:5, 6
> "Trust in the Lord with all your heart, and lean not on your own understanding; in all your ways acknowledge Him, and He shall direct your paths" (NKJV).

and the poor had become destitute. Finding ways to merely survive became a full-time effort. I feared that Russia would return to hard-core communism—ultimate social controls and religious persecution. We were tired of the constant uncertainty. We longed with desperation for economic stability and religious freedom. For many, survival meant leaving Russia behind and moving thousands of miles to the other side of the world—the United States of America. The words inscribed on a plaque near the Statue of Liberty were like a beacon of hope to so many disenfranchised Russians: "Give me your tired, your poor, your teaming masses longing to breathe free." We were tired, we were poor. We longed for a new life. So began a mass exodus from my homeland; an exodus that included many members of my family and friends.

In the space of seven years, nearly my entire family embarked upon a new life in the United States. My sister, Nadia, and her husband, Yuri, immigrated in 1989. They told us of a life filled with promise and a bright future. This prompted my sisters, Lubov and

Lilya, to make the move in 1992. In 1993, my mother, my grand-mother, Antonina, and my brothers, Andrew and Peter, left Russia behind and traveled to a new life in America. My sister, Maria, and her husband, Paul, immigrated to the US in 1996. Nadia, her husband, Yuri, and the rest of my family adopted Fresno, California as their new home. (Several years later, Nadia and Yuri moved to upstate New York; everyone else stayed in Fresno.)

Vasily and I applied for immigration based on religious persecution, as had the rest of my family. With my background as a member of the Baptist Church, obtaining permission was an easy process. Vasily's grandfather had been a born again believer and was imprisoned because of his faith; this background was sufficient for Vasily to receive approval to immigrate. As 1997 began, Vasily and I prepared to take our little ones and begin a new life in a new land.

Although I yearned for the hopeful future that the United States represented, leaving my homeland behind was like tearing away part of my soul. I loved the land of my birth; but the Russia of my youth existed no longer. A future in the US was filled with unknowns and, at once, seemed terrifying and wonderful. We did not know the language and neither of us had jobs. The culture was foreign to us. But we set our eyes on this incredible land that welcomed immigrants from all over the world. Our hearts were filled with dreams of a better life for our little ones.

Several days before our departure date, Vasily went to see a hypnotist. He wanted to have the suggestion implanted in his mind that he no longer preferred to drink. This showed me that my husband truly wanted to find a better life. For a short time, it seemed the hypnotherapy had worked. But I was skeptical; the past had taught me a great deal of caution, even cynicism, where Vasily was concerned.

The day finally arrived—May 26, 1997. With equal amounts of sorrow and delight, we boarded the plane that would fly us into our future. Seven-month-old Peter slept peacefully in my arms for most of the flight to New York. Seven-year-old Aleksey and four-year-old Alexander were wide-eyed with excitement. They giggled through childish conversations and guzzled soda with childish glee. Even the flight attendant was joking about how much soda they drank; for my boys, the sparkling beverage was a rare treat. Through all the miles of that long flight, it seemed we must be the happiest people on the planet.

From New York, we flew to California; there we would begin an entirely new life in Fresno with my mother and grandmother, Antonina. Only those who have entered this land filled with hopes of freedom of speech and religion will understand the golden dreams we had as we arrived at our final destination. Only those who have suffered intense poverty in another land could possibly grasp the utter joy of immigrating to America—the land where anything is possible and even poverty can appear as plenty. As my feet first touched the land of my new home, my heart was filled with a gratitude that overwhelmed any uncertainty or fear.

Immigrating to a new land is one of the most difficult things anyone can undertake. So much of one's identity is tied to the life you live—your job, your friends, your activities. As an immigrant, you leave all those things behind. Probably the most challenging obstacle to overcome is the feeling of being inadequate. Not knowing the language causes others to treat you as though you are not intelligent. New customs and expectations cause you to feel completely isolated among a sea of strangers. In Russia, we had enjoyed respect for our professional skills. In America, we were simply immigrants and the treatment we received was often completely degrading.

For us, the worst part of being immigrants was being totally dependent upon the government for everything. We were allowed five years in which to assimilate into our new home. Until we were able to be self-sufficient, we received a monthly check to pay for our living expenses. It was humiliating to receive a check that I did not work for; it was even more humiliating to have to cash that check and receive the barely concealed looks of pity or disgust. I had worked hard for fourteen years and earned my way through life. It was a powerful blow to my pride when I had to accept charity from a foreign land. The shame I felt paled in comparison to the embarrassment and indignity Vasily suffered. He had been a well-known and respected camera repairman in Russia. In the U.S., he was simply an immigrant living on welfare.

Aleksey and Alexander quickly learned to speak English and seemed to easily blend into life in their new home; not so for me and Vasily. We learned the language one word at a time, one phrase at a time; one sentence at a time. We learned the culture one moment, one mistake, one blunder at a time. Everything was an uphill battle.

Near the end of that first year, the challenge proved too much for Vasily. He surrendered to his old demons and resumed his obsession with alcohol. Where he found the money for it I will never know. But I remember saying to him, "You cannot run away from yourself. Your sin has found you here in America."

After he began to drink again, Vasily returned to his irritable, demanding ways. He would obsess over the tiniest, imagined problems; they would consume him until only the problem filled his mind and heart.

About this time, Vasily started to employ a new tactic against me: he often told Aleksey and Alexander that I was a bad and dangerous person who could not be trusted. Seeing the questions and seeds of distrust in their little eyes was a pain like I had never known. More and more, Vasily would start senseless, unfounded quarrels in front of them; all the while, manipulating them into thinking I was the one at fault.

I knew it was the beginning of the end when Vasily flew into a rage one night nearly a year after we had moved to the U.S. His anger was caused by some trivial disagreement; he pushed me roughly to the couch and held me down with all his might. I realized in that moment that Vasily had chosen his path—alcohol; the resulting anger and violence had won. I knew if he hit me again, I would simply wither away. So I managed to push Vasily from me. Then I grabbed little Peter in my arms and ran for the door, shouting over my shoulder, "I can't live this way anymore!" I heard his footsteps behind me and knew if he caught me, I would suffer at his hands. I ran out the door and through the adjoining yards of the neighborhood. Though I worried about Aleksey and Alexander being left behind, I had to put distance between me and my abuser. My mind raced and my heart pounded from fear and the exertion of carrying 2-year-old Peter. I didn't know where I could go; so I ran through the shadows crying and praying and holding little Peter close. Then I saw Vasily's van moving slowly down the street. I knew he was looking for me. I hid between two buildings and waited. Lena, a friend of mine lived only two blocks from our apartment and I could see her building from my hiding place. Vasily's van stopped in front of her building and he walked to the door. Moments later, I watched him return to the van and drive slowly off down the street. Since Vasily had already looked for me there, I knew her apartment would be a safe refuge for me and Peter. I knocked on her door and she let me in. I was so depressed and so very weary of the traumatic life I lived. Lena and I talked until I calmed somewhat. Then I returned home.

That night, Vasily came to our room and told me he was glad I was home. He asked me to forgive him. But something deep inside me changed irrevocably that night—I had had enough.

The next morning, Vasily told me he would be taking Aleksey and Alexander with him for the day. Apparently, the children had told their father they were afraid to stay at home with me. Vasily's attempt to poison the children against me was working. This was the last drop in an already over-filled cup. I didn't say a word; I simply waited until he had gone and began packing my and the boys' belongings. When I finished, I left our apartment with Peter and hurried to my mother's home. It was June—one year since our immigration to the land of promise. I filed a restraining order against Vasily and started the proceedings for a legal separation.

Somehow, I still hoped that the finality of a legal separation would shock Vasily into reality. Maybe watching all we had worked for fall to pieces would be enough to make him stop drinking and bring understanding to his confused mind.

It seemed for a while that my hopes might be realized. Vasily stopped drinking immediately after he learned I had filed for a separation. Vasily, always the consummate actor, convinced most of our friends and my church family that he had truly changed. When he wanted to, he could be one of the most charming, gracious people I had ever seen. He had a way of making people believe he was broken-hearted at his own failures. He was incredibly adept at manipulating people's thoughts and feelings to his own advantage. How well I knew his talent for softening hearts and altering perceptions. He was a master! And in the mastery of his craft, he had convinced friends and church family alike that I was unreasonably refusing him a second chance.

In short order, the legal separation and restraining order were enacted. Then a nightmare of a whole new sort began; the battle over custody developed all the earmarks of an all-out war. Vasily continued to lie to the children, claiming that I was an angry and dangerous person. He used psychological abuse to turn them against me. He would ask them questions about my actions, my friends, my activities. I begged him to keep our little ones out of the battle; they had been hurt enough. But Vasily was on a mission—a mission to get his way at any cost.

I was granted temporary custody of the children. Then began a never-ending series of court hearings and mediations to decide permanent custody arrangements. At each hearing, Vasily would show up looking the picture of a dignified father—polished and shining and horribly misunderstood. With his charm and cunning intelligence, Vasily convinced nearly everyone that he was being maligned by a vengeful woman.

During the course of the hearings, I made it very clear to everyone that when Vasily was drunk his behavior could become bizarre and extremely dangerous.

Late one evening, I was sitting alone in the living room of my apartment when suddenly I thought I heard something on the roof. I tensed. Then, unmistakably, I heard footsteps overhead. Someone *was* on the roof! I quickly locked the door and shut and secured the latch on the kitchen window. Then I ran to the telephone and called my sister who lived nearby in another one of the apartments. Moments later, I heard a gentle knock at the door. It was Maria and my mother. I let them in and we decided to call the police. By then all was quiet and nothing more happened that evening. But the incident left me tense and anxious.

Throughout the hearings, I was very candid with my attorney

and told him of the many violent episodes in Russia; I told him of the likelihood that Vasily had killed a man shortly before we immigrated. My lawyer spoke seriously of opening a case in Russia to investigate this incident. This subject came up in the court hearings. Vasily realized that facing murder charges in Russia was a distinct possibility that could lead to deportation and imprisonment. Things were beginning to get very serious and the pressure was building against Vasily. This had to have a major impact on his thinking; the specter of his past was rising to haunt him. It had destroyed our family and murder charges loomed before his eyes.

Under a temporary custody agreement, Vasily and I were given equal custody of our boys. The judge said Vasily had never shown violence against the children and the restraining order assured my safety. I begged the judge that Vasily's visits with the children be supervised because of his alcoholism and violent nature. The judge answered that we would revisit the issue if Vasily should endanger the children in any way. 50/50 custody was decreed. The boys would spend one week with me and the next with their father. Dread settled over me at those words.

Vasily continued to beg me to reconsider and forgive him "one last time." But his pleas fell on ears deafened by years of physical, psychological and mental abuse. His lies to the judge about me only served to seal the fate of our marriage. For me, it was over! But for my devastated children, it was an on-going source of pain. They loved both of us and continually begged that things could go back to the way they were. How can a mother's heart listen to the cries of her children and not wish to take away the source of their pain? I considered taking Vasily back for their sake.

But then some more things happened that gave me an uneasy feeling. One Friday evening, when I came to pick up the boys from Vasily, he came to the door with a long-bladed knife in one hand and a sharpening iron in the other. In one eye he wore the monocle he had used as a camera repairman. He drew the knife across the steel slowly and deliberately. The night in Yalta when he had held a knife to my throat for hours flashed through my mind; the sight of him slowly sharpening the knife sent chills down my spine.

On another occasion, I tossed and turned for hours debating with myself whether I should end the legal separation proceedings and go back to Vasily. I fell asleep asking the Lord to lead me.

That night, I dreamed I was running in fear from a man who wished to harm me. I realized I was near my husband's apartment; so I looked through the window and saw him cooking at the stove. He looked at me through the window. All the trouble between us passed through my mind; but I was confident that, in spite of everything, Vasily would protect me from the man who pursued me. Vasily came out of the house carrying a paper bag. He reached in and removed a large stone. I awoke just as he was rushing toward me with murder in his eyes. The Lord had answered my prayer by confirming in my mind the danger Vasily represented.

That morning, I told my family of my dream. They all agreed that the dream was a warning from the Lord. My mind was set and my heart was at peace with the decision to end my marriage. One step at a time, I walked toward what I hoped would be a brighter future for my children and me.

Life Lesson 7 – Hopeful Pathway

Hopes, dreams, values—these are what drive our lives; they provide us with meaning and purpose. Coming to America and all it entailed to live as immigrants in a new land seemed worth the price we paid. I had a dream of a better life in which I would have the freedom to hold fast to my hopes and maintain my values. The greatest of all freedoms was available on these shores—I could worship my God in all ways at all times. I followed a pathway to freedom when I came to the United States.

I often wonder what might have happened had I followed a pathway to freedom rather than remaining in an abusive marriage. I strongly question if the pathway I followed in marrying Vasily was God's will for me. He provided so many ways of escape both before and after our marriage; yet I chose to ignore them all. I wonder too, if my marriage was even recognized as a marriage by God. It is not my wish to bring up weighty theological questions or give rise to debate. But the relationship between me and Vasily failed at every turn and at every point to embody a true marriage. As I understand it, marriage is the merging of two separate people into one being. Only God can accomplish this feat. Vasily and I were never together in the Lord. We never exchanged vows before God. How could we have ever become one?

After years of being continually beaten down and mired in dark chaos, I finally realized the hope I had maintained for my marriage was not hope at all. It was only a possibility that required an act of free will—from both me and my husband. Bit-by-bit through the years of turmoil, I learned what my mind did not want to accept. It was much like learning the English language as a Russian immigrant. Traditions, adages, sayings, slang—it's all foreign and incomprehensible to one with a different past. You have to know the culture to understand so much of the language. One fact of American culture at a time is stored in your memory; and one phrase at a time begins to make sense. In time, your vocabulary is enlarged and you no longer struggle to understand. Just so, I came to the place where I understood Vasily and I spoke entirely different languages. It took many years for me to finally understand the culture inside our very beings was totally and irreconcilably unrelated. We lived two vastly different realities and would never speak the same language.

We have the Lord's promise that He will direct our paths; but that promise has a condition—"in all your ways acknowledge Him." How many times did I ignore the leading of God? How many times did I choose my own path rather than the one He desired for me? How much agony did I cause myself by stubbornly holding to a false hope?

From the depths of my being I now cry with David, "Show me Your ways, O Lord; teach me Your paths" (Psalm 25:4; NKJV). It is only in this dependent state that we can truly walk the paths God has ordained for each of us. This Psalm goes on to say "Lead me in Your truth and teach me, for You are the God of my salvation" (Psalm 25:5; NKJV). It is only when we sacrifice our own independence and rely totally on Him that we gain wisdom and knowledge to lead us to the abundant life God desires for each of us.

Consider this:
1. In what ways have you stubbornly refused to veer from the course you chose rather than follow the Lord's leading?
2. What were the repercussions of choosing your own path rather than following the Lord?
3. What do you perceive to be the difference between "trust[ing] in the Lord" and leaning on your own understanding?
4. What does it mean to acknowledge God in all your ways?
5. In what ways has your determination to follow your own course brought sorrow and pain into your life?
6. Joel 2:25 says, "So I will restore to you the years that the swarming locust has eaten" (NKJV). What do you believe this means for your own life?

Chapter 8

Shattered Hope

It was the beginning of a new year—1999. We were still in the midst of the legal proceedings. Vasily continued begging me to take him back; I continued to hold fast to my decision. My children and I needed security and peace. With Vasily, neither of those could be found.

It was around this time

> Matthew 7
> "But everyone who hears these sayings of Mine, and does not do them, will be like a foolish man who built his house on the sand: and the rain descended, the floods came, and the winds blew and beat on that house; and it fell. And great was its fall" (NKJV).

that the children and I began to form a very special bond. I tried to help them understand the reasons for the separation and let them ask questions and voice their concerns. I remember 9-year-old Aleksey saying in his most serious little boy voice, "Mommy, I don't want to live on this earth anymore. There is too much pain; too much crying. I want to go to heaven and be with God. I want to see my older brother Dennis and play with him." My heart shattered that my little boy had reached the point where he despaired of this life. I held him and tried to soothe his innocent, broken heart. I told him he was too young to have such thoughts. I encouraged him to believe everything would turn out well because God loved him. I explained that there is a time for everything under the sun; and one day, he would be in heaven with his older brother. I tried to help him understand that we must live every day in the best way we can and allow God to plan our futures. Life had created such heavy burdens for one so young. I hid my tears and hugged him tight. If only I could have taken away his pain.

With all the stress that piled higher daily, I began the new year by contracting a vicious virus. A high fever made me feel as though I walked underwater and my throbbing head made even the simplest of chores nearly unbearable. I visited the doctor and got a prescription to combat the infection. The difficulties of being a single mother came into sharper focus as I faced taking all three boys to the mall to get the prescription filled.

As we entered the mall, we heard the happy strains of a calliope in the center court; the sound drew the boys toward the carousel. All three began begging me to let them ride. It was a magnificent carousel, trimmed with gold decorations and glowing with lights. Three rows of brightly painted horses circled under the purple and white awning. Although the mere act of walking was nearly more than I could endure, I could not tell them "no." I purchased tickets and leaned against a nearby wall as the boys scampered up onto the prancing ponies. Their giggles echoed through the expanse, nearly drowning out the carousel music.

It was so wonderful to see my children so happy after so many months of confusion and pain. My boys were just little children—much too young to understand the dynamics surrounding the separation. They only knew their family had been broken and their sad little eyes had lost the sparkle that had once lit them from within. The traumatic drama of the past months faded to the background as my heart absorbed the beauty of their laughter.

The young girl operating the carousel was quite taken by the obvious unrestrained joy of my boys. She asked me if she could keep them on for the next ride. I explained to her that I needed to get a prescription filled quickly. She must have realized just how sick I was; she offered to allow the kids to ride without tickets until I returned. I was overwhelmed at such generosity and kindness. With one more loving look at my happy boys, I hurried off to get the much-needed medicine.

When I returned, my boys were still in the throes of absolute glee. I have no idea how many times they circled on that carousel, riding their white, black, and brown ponies; but their little eyes were twinkling and their grins outshined the rides' vibrant display. I thanked God for allowing my little ones such an unexpected treat and we left the mall filled with the glow of delight. It was a time of lighthearted fun in the midst of turmoil and sorrow. Such a precious memory!

On January 17th, in compliance with the temporary custody arrangement the courts had decreed, I turned the children over to Vasily. Alternating weeks with Vasily was proving to be extremely difficult. I worried about my sons the entire time they were with their dad. But the boys loved him and were delighted to be spending time with him. Every time he picked them up they practically bowled him over with their enthusiastic greetings. On this day, Vasily seemed subdued, even a bit distracted when he arrived to pick up the boys. I convinced myself his uncharacteristic restraint was due to the fact that our legal separation would soon be final. The boys gave me kisses and hugs and left with their little suitcases in tow. I heard them chattering happily all the way down the hall.

There was an important court hearing on January 19th. The judge handling our case was absent that day, and a woman substitute was there in his place. Vasily acted very strangely throughout the proceedings; he seemed agitated and unfocused. He continued to blame me and my family for all the problems in our marriage. The substitute judge wasn't familiar with our case and Vasily's vehement claims finally swayed her in his favor. I begged the judge to make Vasily's visits with the children supervised because of his alcoholism and violent nature. The judge answered that we would revisit the issue if Vasily should endanger the children in any way. In the end, she upheld the temporary custody agreement and awarded Vasily and I equal custody—he would have them one week and I would have them the next. I felt helpless. I felt fearful.

The legal separation was final and now I faced life as a single mother in a new land with a mixture of hope and apprehension. I still held in reserve the option to make the separation a divorce, wondering if the separation would motivate Vasily to get help and make real and permanent changes in his life. I could not pull back the veil and see into tomorrow; I could only do my best and trust that God would guide my steps.

That week without my little ones seemed endless and devoid of life. I spoke with them each night on the phone; but my arms ached to hold them and my eyes hungered to see their cute little faces. I missed them with every fiber of my being. I counted the days until 6:00 p.m., Friday, January 22nd, the day my little angels would come home.

On Thursday, January 21st, I tried to call the boys numerous times; but the phone only rang and rang. As the day wore on, I became more and more distraught.

To make matters worse, my Grandmother, Antonina, grew gravely ill. We rushed her to the emergency room that afternoon and were told she was suffering from severe pneumonia. The prognosis was grim. The doctor told us the infection had reached her bloodstream and she would not recover. We brought her home and made her as comfortable as possible. My heart ached for my precious grandmother. I could not imagine life without her wise and comforting presence.

Finally, at about 11:00 p.m. on Thursday night, Vasily answered his phone. I was irate! I demanded he let me speak to the boys. It seemed he didn't even hear my words. He only asked, "Tell me, do you forgive me or not." I was appalled that he could even ask the question when I was so upset. I demanded to talk to the boys and Vasily insisted I answer his question. Filled with frustrated anger, I slammed the phone down and sobbed out my worry and irritation. I decided I would go to Vasily's apartment the next day and pick up my boys. I just didn't trust he would bring them home.

Vasily called repeatedly throughout Thursday night and into the wee hours of Friday morning. The first couple of times I answered. He asked me why I no longer loved him or our children. I was stunned! My world revolved around my sons. How was it possible the man I had shared life with for so many years knew so little about me? I told Vasily I could not simply let him return. I needed time to make sure he had changed. He responded, "There is no more time." I thought his words strange and unsettling, but I would have the boys with me the next day. I was completely exhausted, both physically and emotionally. I finally unplugged the phone. I had to get some sleep before another work day began.

Looking back, I realize I failed to see just how desperate Vasily had become. I did not see that I was pushing his deranged, frightened, and depressed mind into a place of no return. I did not understand that Vasily spoke the truth when he told me time had run out.

Early the morning of January 22nd, I got up for work. I called Vasily, asking him to let me speak with the children. He refused; he only continued trying to convince me to take him back. His voice seemed very strange; he sounded hollow and very depressed. I asked him if the boys were in school. His response seemed totally nonsensical: "You know." Rather than listen to further badgering, I hung up the phone.

On my way to work, I stopped by the children's school and found they had not attended for the past three days. I was livid! Determining to have a stern talk with Vasily after work, I rushed to my grandmother's bedside. I knew I could talk with Vasily and the school another day, but any moment could be my grandmother's last on earth. I spent as much time as I could with Grandma and then, with a burdened heart, I drove to the Fresno Shirt Company and began a long and grueling workday.

The more I thought about the boys not being in school, the more frantic I became. I recalled Vasily's strange demeanor on the phone. He had seemed so disconnected from reality ... so vacant and detached. Horrific thoughts flitted through my mind leaving more panic in their wake. I finally called my sister and asked her to contact the police and ask them to check on the boys. It wasn't long before my sister called back and told me all was well. The police officer had inspected the apartment and seen all three boys were safe and sound. Vasily had showed the officer a bottle of medicine and told her the boys had missed school because of a bad cold. With this report, I calmed somewhat; but I still felt a sense of foreboding. I could not wait for that day to end and my boys to be back in my arms.

It was about noon when I received the dreaded call from my sister. My grandmother had gone on to heaven and this earth was poorer for her passing. A rock formed in my throat. How could she be gone? I had just talked with her that morning! Tears streamed down my face as prayers streamed from my lips. My already burdened little boys would now be told their beloved great-grandmother had passed from this life and now resided in heaven. How could they handle yet another loss? I worried about Aleksey. He had already told me he'd rather be in heaven. What affect would this news have on his wounded little heart?

My heart was nearly overwhelmed with opposing emotions as I left work and went with my brother-in-law to pick up my boys: joy at being reunited with my children and grief at the loss that day had brought. On the drive to Vasily's apartment, I rehearsed how I would tell the boys of their great-grandmother's death. I knew I wanted to stress to them that the separation was only for a time. One day, we would all live together in a perfect land without any pain or loss or suffering or death. One day, we would all be together in God's heaven.

Flashing red lights caught my attention as we neared the street leading to Vasily's apartment. The way was blocked by a multitude of police cars. I explained to a police officer that I had come to get my boys and they let us through. The entire street was lined with vehicles; the revolving lights turned the night into a bizarre and eerie kaleidoscope. A helicopter hovered above the street dragging a search light as it went. Throngs of people milled about in front of the apartment building. Television crews filmed the ghastly scene. Firemen rushed about and police officers patrolled the area. The entire scene felt horrifyingly surreal. An all-encompassing fear began to grow until it threatened to strangle all breath from my body.

We finally reached the driveway into the apartment complex. Shock waves pulsed through my being as I realized a fire raged in Vasily's building. My world exploded when the truth dawned— smoke was pouring out of the window of my boys' room as flames lapped at the walls!

I jumped from the car and careened toward the building. A panic I had never known seized my being and pushed all logic aside.

As I rushed toward the entrance, I saw Vasily's couch sitting on the lawn next to Peter's bicycle. Blinded by smoke and fear, I pushed my way through the throng of people. I had to get to my boys! Suddenly, my brother-in-law grabbed me by my shoulders and spun me to face him. Looking into my eyes, he said, "No! Stop!" His words tore something loose inside me and I began to scream, "I need to check on my children! I need to check on my children!" Why couldn't he understand? His strong arms held me in place as my eyes darted and my heart raced.

I wondered if the children could be among the throng of people who surrounded the dreadful scene. I frantically scanned the crowd. I saw a man walking toward me. The look on his face sent my mind reeling and brought new terror to my heart. He stopped before me and asked, "Who is the mother of the children?" I don't remember answering him; I only remember his next words, "I am sorry, ma'am. I am very sorry. We've just found three bodies inside. We weren't able to identify them but they are all dead. We aren't able to tell you if all three of the bodies found are those of children. There may be one adult and two children. But all are deceased."

I screamed, "I want to die!" and then felt myself collapse. My world stopped. Everything around me grew dark and dim. I saw faces—my mother, my sisters, others I did not know. I heard voices but I could not decipher the meanings of their words. I could not believe any of the circumstances around me were real. I had to be in some nightmare, some alternate reality that would soon fade away. This could not be happening! Everything fragmented. I wanted life to end. I was vaguely aware of being placed on a gurney. People of all sorts, tangles of words, cameras, monitors, a police officer sitting in a chair—I saw but I did not comprehend.

Deep inside, I clung to the threadbare hope that one of my precious boys still lived. I hoped against hope that the body of Vasily was the third set of remains. Oh, that God would grant me the desperate plea that one of my little sons had survived.

Sometime later, I found myself in a police car being escorted to my sister's home. During the drive, the officer received a call. We pulled into the apartment complex and parked. The officer turned to me, a deep sadness etching his face. As compassionately as possible, he told me all three of my boys had burned to death in the fire. Vasily's body had been found in a grassy area two blocks away. He had died of blood loss.

I was unable to breathe ... there was nothing to breathe.

All I recall of the rest of that night is pain ... and tears ... and more pain. Tears rolled down my face in a hot, salty flood; they pooled in my ears and soaked my pillow. And still, more tears came.

Life Lesson 8 – Shattered Hope

It is nearly impossible to convey with mere words the extent of the hellish agony that exploded my world that horrible night. My embattled mind and heart reeled with the onslaught of grief, disbelief, regret, despair, torment, mourning, rage.

I now read the words of Job and realize the full extent of his meaning: "Why then have You brought me out of the womb? Would that I had died and no eye had seen me! 'I should have been as though I had not been, carried from womb to tomb" (Job 10:18, 19; NKJV). I too came to wish I had never been born.

But underneath all the cacophony of emotions laid the bedrock of guilt—my own. In my disobedience to and rebellion against God, I had built my house on sand. And the storms of life had swept it away as surely as if it had never been.

Thankfully, the life repercussions of ungodly choices rarely reach the magnitude of the bomb that detonated in my own. However, when God's people freely choose to place themselves in the enemy's campground, the consequences will come. At these times, it is often tempting to blame God. But our heavenly Father never changes. He is love at all times and in all ways. The consequences we face for our disobedience are consequences we set in place by our own free will. Because of His limitless love, God doesn't interfere with our freedom to choose. We are responsible for our own choices and must bear the weight of the resulting events.

I do not wish to proclaim some name-it-and-claim-it theology. Nor does God operate on a system of punishment and reward in order to gain our love and obedience. God operates only in love; and because of that love, He provides for our every need. But as His people, we must choose each moment whether we will place ourselves in the path of blessing or position ourselves in the way of curse. To walk in the ways of the Lord will always bring blessing (Proverbs 3:5, 6). To travel the path of the enemy will always bring curse (Psalm 1).

As we have seen repeatedly throughout these chapters, our enemy, satan, seeks to kill, steal, and destroy. He hates God's people and awaits any opportunity to rain down his loathing. We must guard against his devices and schemes. We must run to our Lord for He is our refuge from the wiles of the devil. Only in Him will we find rest for our souls, abundant life in this world, and eternal life with Him when our time on earth is done.

Consider this:

1. What emotions are stirred within you by the recounting of this horrific series of events?
2. What are your thoughts regarding God in light of what you have just read?
3. Do you find it difficult to reconcile a loving God with the heart-wrenching death of the three innocent boys?
4. At what point in your life did you suffer the negative consequences of your own ungodly choices?
5. In what ways did you struggle to accept the consequences while remaining convinced of God's love?
6. Read Romans 8:28. What are your thoughts regarding this truth in light of the story you just read?
7. If you know Job's story, read chapters 38 through 41. If you are not familiar with the story of Job, you may wish to take time to read the book, concentrating on the final four chapters. How do these chapters impact your understanding of suffering?

Chapter 9

Eternal Hope

The morning after my little ones had passed from this life, I returned to my apartment. My sister, Nadia, who had already arrived from New York, stayed by my side as I unlocked the door and walked inside. Scattered here and there were the boys' toys,

drawings, jackets … each tiny article was like a blade to my heart. Only days before, my home had been filled with the voices and laughter of my precious sons; now only silence echoed from room to room.

Somewhere beyond the silence, I could still hear the laughter of that golden day at the mall—all three boys giggling and shouting their joy as the carousel carried them on that last enchanted ride. My mind filled with images of their sparkling eyes and joyful smiles. I felt a smile turn the corners of my own mouth before realization crashed upon my soul anew. The inconceivable reality fell on my heart like a fiery rain, obliterating my soul and setting my mind ablaze with images of what was … and what would never again be. How could my sons be gone from me?

I felt more dead than alive as I walked through the home I had shared with my sons. Nine-year-old Aleksey's jacket still hung crookedly on the back of the chair where he had flung it days before. Six-year-old Alexander's toys were piled in a corner where he had stashed them. And little two-year-old Peter's latest drawing hung on the refrigerator; he had been so proud of his artwork.

Every step, every item, every breath brought a new surge of suffocating pain. When my little ones needed me most, I was not there. I had fought to protect them ... I had failed. And my precious sons had paid the price of my failure. I wanted to trade places with them! I wanted to scream; I wanted to run from a reality too horrifying to accept; I wanted to simply stop living.

Emotions careened in my heart as thoughts and images collided in my mind. I begged God to end my life; for a life without my sons was no life at all. How could I walk through empty, purposeless days when my children had been taken from me? I had lost all will and reason to live. Yet my mutilated heart continued beating and each pain-wracked breath was evidence that my life went on.

A stream of people poured into my little apartment that day— friends with condolences, relatives with tear-stained faces, reporters with cameras, officials with paperwork, and doctors with offers of medication. Filled with good intentions, their presence only added chaos to my grief.

At some point during that endless day, the detective investigating the tragedy sat down beside me on the couch. His face was grim as he told me the horrific truth they had uncovered. He told me my boys had died before the fire ever began. In a voice as subdued as the grave, he explained in detail how Vasily had used a knife to kill them, and how he had carried their little bodies to their own beds and doused them with gasoline. After that, he set the fire and ran from the apartment. In a quiet, dark place, two blocks away, he killed himself in the same gruesome way he had killed the boys. Had they found him only a few minutes sooner, Vasily would most likely have survived.

My soul could not comprehend the horror of my children's last hour. To have the father they loved steal their lives ... how, Lord, how could he have done such a thing? Gruesome images overtook my mind: terror filled little eyes watching as brothers were killed; the man I had once loved overtaken by pure, unbridled evil; the blood of my precious little boys. Their still little forms after Vasily's gruesome act of violence. It was too much! How could anyone live with such knowledge? How could I go on?

My being was filled with a hideous feeling of responsibility. I felt wholly accountable for the death of my little ones. If I had not left Vasily, he would not have had the final meltdown that led to the cruel murder of innocent lives. Had I remained with him and accepted his abuse, my children would have been spared. But I had wanted freedom; I had wanted an end to the traumatic life we had lived. However, freedom at the cost of all I held dear seemed no freedom at all. It was only bondage to a pain that would pulse in my being for the rest of my days.

I have little memory of the days leading up to the funeral. Vague images of people's faces and disconnected words were like specters from another dimension, never truly entering my world. I had cried so many tears that the well of my grief was empty. I moved through that time in a haze of disbelief. Emotions too overwhelming to face pummeled my heart until only a numb void remained. The minutes ticked by, bringing ever-closer the moment when I would have to say my final farewell to my children.

Time ceased to have any meaning for me. I simply existed. I continually rehearsed a litany of "why." Why had God allowed this? Why didn't He stop it? Why didn't He protect my sons? Why did I have to go on living when all meaning and purpose had been taken from me? The lack of answers from my heavenly Father threatened to crush me beneath a weight of silence.

The day arrived. From some unknown reservoir of strength, I managed to accompany my family to the church for the funeral service. At the front of the large sanctuary was a cascade of flowers and three white caskets. In an open casket lay my beloved grandmother, Antonina. The grief of losing her had been so overshadowed by the death of my three children that I had nearly forgotten death had also claimed her. Standing over her still form brought fresh torrents of tears. I had loved her so very much. To the left of my grandmother's body stood a closed casket. Deep within its satiny folds laid the body of my firstborn, my Aleksey. To the right of my grandmother, another closed casket held the bodies of my littlest ones, Alexander and Peter. They were so tiny; only one coffin held them both.

My sister, Nadia, walked beside me as I neared the boys' caskets. I had not seen their faces since they left my side for the last time over a week before. I knew this was the only chance I would have to gaze upon their faces—before the time of visitation began. I placed my finger beneath the lid of Aleksey's coffin. I whispered to Nadia, "I cannot believe my children are really in there. I need to see them or I will never be able to accept this." My sister simply asked, "How will you go on with your life?" Her response reminded me of the advice of others: if I saw the state of their little bodies, I would never be able to face the rest of life. After a few moments of struggle, I decided I would rather remember them full of life and energy and excitement. I wanted to hold fast to the memory of their beautiful faces, their eyes, their smiles. I wanted to forever see them as they were on the carousel—vibrantly alive and filled with childlike joy.

All during the funeral, I stared into the emptiness my world had become. People spoke of my loved ones, sang beloved hymns, prayed impassioned prayers, recited heart-felt poems, and cried out their grief while I sat in a daze—deaf and blind to the world around me. Then the service ended. It was time to say goodbye. I rose from my seat and approached the caskets. Words ripped from my heart; "My dear, sweet babies! How will I ever go on without you? Vasily, how could you have done this?!" I laid my head on the nearest casket and felt waves of grief crash in the deepest parts of my heart and soul. I could not bring myself to walk away.

Just as I felt my own life would end from the severity of my pain, someone came beside me, hugged me, and joined me in my cries of agony. I looked up; and through a veil of tears I saw my mother—my dearest mother who had lost her own mother and three grandchildren in the same hellish day. She held me close as I sobbed out my love and final goodbye to Aleksey, Alexander, and Peter. As she supported my trembling frame, we walked out of the church and into the darkest sun-filled day my world had ever held.

A motorcade awaited us, led by a long black limousine. A dozen policemen on motorcycles sat silently as the mourners entered their cars; the policemen escorted us through the streets as the procession began. The long line of vehicles drove slowly to the cemetery. The caskets were placed under a large, white tent where the interment service was held. It was attended by a huge crowd, including members of the press. Finally, the coffins were lowered into the graves. The pain that flooded my heart echoed across that graveyard as a fresh outburst of tears was wrung from a sea of broken hearts. The finality was excruciating; but I knew my boys were already in heaven with their Grandma. (I believe that God graciously took Grandma first, on the very same day, so she would be there to welcome my boys, together with my own Daddy, at the gates of heaven with Jesus.)

Vasily was to be cremated. I had an overwhelming urge to see his body. Nadia went with me to the morgue. We found his body lying on a table, covered by a sheet from the waist down; a towel was draped over his head. The condition of his body was frightful; his face and hands were covered in angry blisters. In that moment, I fully grasped the identity of the true villain. satan, the father of all evil, had overtaken Vasily and, as a master puppeteer, the enemy of our souls had engineered this heinous crime. Feelings of regret and pity overtook me. Miraculously, I felt a stream of mercy flood my being—a gift from my Comforter, my Redeemer, my God. Standing there above Vasily's mutilated body I felt chains fall from my being—chains that had been forged by fourteen years of heartbreak and abuse. Fear and dread fell from my heart like discarded scales. I was free of this man, the one I had once loved, the father of my babies, the killer of my children. Vasily's body was prepared for cremation; but where was his soul?

When Vasily's ashes were placed in the urn, only my sister, Nadia, and I were present. His ashes were buried in a cemetery far from the children. I placed a carnation with a broken stem on Vasily's grave. It was a symbol of the choices Vasily had made to shatter his own life.

My heart was filled with true sorrow for Vasily. He had so many chances to change his life; he was granted so many opportunities to meet Jesus, the only One who could give him a new heart and a new life. He had listened to the demons that terrorized him and finally drove him to a monstrous level of madness. Vasily was a deceived victim of satan; and God gave me a supernatural ability to let the healing power of forgiveness begin to flow. By a powerful act of God, I forgave my abuser and the murderer of my children.

In the days that followed, I spent many hours at the cemetery. My tears watered my children's graves. I knew my innocent angels awaited our reunion on the other side of eternity; but the ache in my soul was unrelenting. One particularly pain-wracked day when I was at the gravesite, my prayers were interrupted by a kind and peaceful voice speaking very distinctly and clearly in my soul: "Galina, I love you very much." I could not mistake the voice of my Lord and Savior. "Don't cry for your children. They are with me and no one can ever harm them again. They are happy with me today. And, one day, you will be with them forever." An incredible peace welled up within me. "I have a plan for you, Galina. I am with you." Then I heard another voice; it was unmistakably that of Aleksey, speaking in the same way—very distinctly and clearly in my soul. He also encouraged me, "Mom, don't cry for us. We are so happy here with Jesus."

From that moment, peace reigned in my heart. Though I still grieved for my children, the peace in my soul was even more powerful than my pain. God had worked a miracle in my heart.

At some point in the traumatic days following my sons' deaths, my sister, Nadia, had told us of a family she knew who had also suffered a great loss. They lived near her in New York, in a small upstate town named Apalachin. A precious, 37-year-old woman, Elsie Messmer, had died suddenly of a heart attack. She was the mother of four children: Eva Marie who was 10, Steven Alexander who was 8, Joshua Charles who was 5, and Jesse Israel who was only 3 years old. Her husband, Peter, was devastated and in dire need of prayer support. Though he was a Christian, his faith had been dealt a severe blow and he was struggling to endure his loss. We were all only too acquainted with the devastating pain of sudden, unexpected death. So we all agreed to pray for this man and his family.

Feeling as though a bomb had obliterated my world, I faced the task of re-entering life. I still had to make a living; and now, I had staggering funeral bills to pay. I am not sure how I managed to force myself to report back to work. On that first day back, I sat behind my sewing machine working on a shirt for the very man who had been the presiding judge over our legal separation and custody case. Rather than anger, I felt only sadness and regret. This man had made a grave error in judgment. I could only wonder how he must be feeling after learning of my children's fate.

The day after the tragedy, the local newspaper had run the story about my children's deaths. As a result, a seemingly endless flood of help rolled in from every direction. Letters of support were sent to me; people prayed on my behalf; others brought food and made necessary phone calls; people I had never met contributed financially. All expenses were covered through the generosity of others. And all my needs were met through the grace and mercy of my Lord.

My boss brought me flowers one day and set them on my sewing machine at work. He told me my children had whispered to him, "Please take flowers to our mother for us. We want to wish a happy Mother's Day to our wonderful mother." I saw the Lord's hand at work in this extraordinary act. Tears of gratitude flowed as I thanked my heavenly Father for His tender mercy and care.

Each morning, I would read the psalms of King David. David had lost his son; he had wept and grieved just as I had. Yet, his love for God never wavered. His trust in his heavenly Father never dimmed. The words of the songs he wrote soothed my soul and quieted my mind. David's faith was a beacon during those first few weeks. I prayed for a heart like his.

Also, during this time, I began to think often about Eve. She was the first mother to experience the pain of losing a child. Eve was also acquainted with the intense sorrow of knowing her child was murdered by one he loved. Yet Eve persevered through her loss and her world kept on turning. Life went on.

So I put one foot in front of the other and carried my broken heart through my days. Tears flowed often and pain was a constant visitor. But God gave me the strength to face each moment as it came. I moved into a one-bedroom apartment, got my driver's license, bought a car, and prepared to face a strange and frighteningly unknown future alone.

One day, my sister, Nadia, called with a strange request. It seems the man who had lost his wife, Peter Messmer, felt talking with me might be a way for both of us to process our grief. I remembered the multitude of letters and cards I had received from strangers and how much the support of others had meant to me. I recalled the words of Scripture that tell us to bear one another's burdens. So I agreed to correspond with this hurting man.

On March 25th, two months after the tragedy, I received the first letter from Peter. Still being far less than fluent with the English language, I took the letter to my sister, Lyuba, so she could translate it for me. His letter was filled with pain-wracked descriptions of his wife's death and the heartbreak he and his children still suffered. His anger at God was glaringly apparent in his anguished words. He demanded answers from God to questions that burned in his soul: How could God allow this to happen? Why would he leave four little children without a mother? Where was God while she was dying? Why hadn't He saved her?

My heart reached out to this hurting family. I wanted to answer Peter's letter; but my command of the English language prevented me. Lyuba graciously offered to translate my Russian letters into English. So I wrote … and wrote. My letter seemed to grow into a many-chaptered book as I poured my heart out and tried to offer encouragement to this grieving man. I had provided an enormous task for Lyuba; but she faithfully translated every word by hand and sent my letter and the English translation to Peter. In very short order, I received another letter from Peter and our pen pal relationship began in earnest.

Thus began the fulfillment of a precious Scriptural promise in my life: "So I will restore to you the years that the swarming locust has eaten" (Joel 2:25).

A gruesome trail

By Michael Krikorian
The Fresno Bee

January 24th, 1999—The father of three young brothers found slain in a charred Fresno apartment was discovered dead from self-inflicted wounds early Saturday and is the prime suspect in the triple murder, police said.

The body of Vasily Petrovich Losev, 45, was discovered on his back with arms outstretched in a grassy vacant lot about a quarter-mile from the Oakwood apartment complex, police said.

Nearly six hours earlier, the bodies of his three sons - Alexi, 9; Alexander, 6; and Peter, 2 - were found in the ruins of Losev's unit after the fire that consumed it was extinguished about 6:15 p.m. Friday.

The boys' mother, Galina Loseva, who is separated from her husband, was coming to pick up the children when the fire erupted at the complex, located near McKinley and Maple avenues.

Family members claim the husband knew his wife was coming for the children, so he killed the boys, then set the fire shortly before she was due to arrive.

"We all know Vasily did it," said Vera Lyubov, one of Galina Loseva's five sisters. "And he wanted her to see it, too."

As flames began to shoot out of the first-floor apartment, the mother arrived and saw the hellish scene.

"She kept yelling, and she started to go in, but they stopped her," said David Hicks, the security guard at the Oakwood Apartments.

Then Galina Loseva collapsed.

Investigators initially considered the possibility that the brothers died from an accidental fire at the apartment complex. But by Saturday, both police and the Fresno County Coroner's Office were ruling the deaths a triple homicide.

"This is a homicide," said detective Al Murrietta, the lead investigator.

Murrietta declined to speculate as to whether the children had been killed before the fire was set.

"We are waiting for the autopsy," he said. "Because of the fire damage to the corpses, we can't say yet. It takes some time."

Witnesses reported seeing a man run from the apartment seconds after the fire broke out in the two-bedroom unit.

Losev's body was found shortly after midnight. A trail, left from his self-inflicted wounds, led police along a sidewalk and through a dirt field to the place where he lay.

"When I saw him, he had blood everywhere," Murrietta said.

Authorities would not say how the wounds were inflicted.

Losev, who was unemployed, had separated from his wife, a seamstress at the Fresno Shirt Co., and the two had joint custody of the boys, friends and relatives said. The wife has an "a" added to the end of her last name, a custom Russians often practice.

The couple, immigrants who arrived in the United States 18 months ago, were married 14 years. They split up six months ago, relatives said.

The boys' mother, already grieving over the Friday afternoon death of her 87-year-old grandmother, was devastated by the deaths of her sons.

"Just as she was starting to grieve over her grandmother, she gets this shock," said her brother-in-law, Tim Heinrichs. "It's too much for anyone. Her eyes are all puffed up from crying all night and all morning today."

Galina, 36, met **Vasily** Losev in 1984 when she went to stay at her family's apartment in the city of Yalta on the Black Sea.

She landed a job as a photographer. Losev was a camera repairman.

"He saw her taking pictures on the beach and thought she was beautiful," Lyubov said. "I wish he never saw her."

Family members described Losev as an abusive husband, irate over the custody battle for the couple's children.

"For the world to see, Vasily was a very pleasant guy, but in private he was a textbook abusive husband," said Heinrichs, an electrician. "He was nice in public, but his private persona was devilish."

Tuesday, the father attended a court hearing on the custody of the children, relatives said.

"Vasily was upset because there was a woman appointed as the commissioner or judge and he didn't like that," Vera Lyubov said.

"He had a strange idea of what it meant to be a man," said Heinrichs, who was acting as a spokesman for the broken-hearted Loseva. "One of the things he had to do was to dominate over everything. The women were like servants."

At the Oakwood complex, young friends of the boys rode bicycles back and forth in front of the gutted, blackened shell that once was an apartment.

"We used to play together all the time," said Crystal Menendez, 12. "They were nice to me. A lot of boys aren't."

Security guard Hicks walked into the charred bedroom where the three brothers played video games, slept and died.

"The kids were really sweet, really well-mannered," said Hicks, whose son played soccer with Alexander. "It's really hard. Kids you see all the time, playing, having fun, and all of a sudden they're gone."

Lyudmila Ivaschenko, a friend of the father, was dumbfounded.

"I just can't believe this," Ivaschenko said as she stood on the field where Losev died. "He was such a nice man. I can't believe he did this. They're all dead."

Plans for a funeral are on hold as family members, who have no insurance, try to raise money to bury five people: the three boys, the grandmother and the father.

"Even though he killed them, we are going to bury them together," Heinrichs said.

At the Coco Palms Apartments where Galina Loseva lives, two young female cousins of the murdered brothers were going through some photo albums.

They smiled and giggled at some of the pictures, lost in memories. They showed off color photographs of the family at a small museum in St. Petersburg, on the beach at Yalta and at the Moscow airport as the smiling family prepared to board a plane for America.

Then the girls remembered Friday night.

"They're angels now," 12-year-old Anastasia Koudriavtseva said, tears filling her eyes.

"They're small angels now. Looking out for everyone. Looking out for me."

A mother's farewell to three sons

By Michael Krikorian
The Fresono Bee

January 30th, 1999—Three young boys, immigrants from Russia to Fresno, should have been comforting their mother Friday as she grieved and watched her grandmother laid to rest on a bright, sun-drenched afternoon. They should have stood near their mom, Galina Loseva, and their aunts and uncles as the matriarch of the family was buried.

But instead of standing with their living family, the boys, ages 9, 6, and 2, were buried alongside their 87-year-old great-grandmother in a ceremony at Clovis Cemetery.

Alexi, Alexander and Peter Losev were the victims of a brutal slaying at the hands of their father eight days ago.

Shortly before their mother was to pick them up Jan. 22, their father, Vasily Losev, killed them with a knife, then set fire to his Fresno apartment. He killed himself a short while later. The boys' mother and father had separated and were in a custody battle.

In a scene as heart-wrenching as any tragic Russian play, Galina Loseva rushed to their small caskets at the end of the service, fell to her knees, sobbed softly and rested the side of her face on the coffins.

More than 250 people, from elderly Russian women with colorful scarfs around their heads to young classmates of the slain children, attended the service at Peoples Church in northeast Fresno. Many carried boxes of tissues.

Flanking the full-sized open casket in which lay Antonina Vysotskaya were two smaller white closed coffins. In one was the body of Alexi Losev, the oldest boy. In the other were the bodies of Alexander and Peter.

"What happened a few days ago shocked the whole city," said Pastor Vyacheslav Tsvirenko of Fresno's Russian Baptist Church.

Tsvirenko contrasted the long life of the great-grandmother with those of the three youngsters.

She was born in 1911 in St. Petersburg. The Russian Revolution erupted when she was 6 years old. By the time she was 30, she was a respected nurse during the legendary battles between the Nazis and Red Army in her hometown, then called Leningrad. She came to America in the early 1990s.

She died of natural causes the same day the boys were murdered.

"At the same time today, we have the bodies of children," Tsvirenko said. "Nine, 6 and 2. What can you do in that time? What can a person see? But in their short lives, they learned the most important lesson. They learned to love God."

Throughout the service, speakers sought to comfort Galina Loseva with the thought that some day she would be reunited with her children.

"Whoever wants to see the boys must live a life that leads them to heaven," said Victor Ivaschenko, a neighbor of the family.

But it was difficult to tell whether Loseva was listening.

"It's so hard to say anything, to hear anything," Loseva said later.

Most of time, Loseva stared blankly. Her eyes were open, but they were not looking at anything.

At the tented grave site, sitting with her mother, sisters and brothers, she showed the pained expression of someone resigned to suffer a horrific nightmare that will not end.

As 18 boys and girls carrying red and pink carnations sang a favorite song of Alexi's, Loseva's sisters, brothers and friends cried.

Loseva shed no tears.

"There are no more tears left in her body," said her sister, Lilia Titar. "Only God is helping us through this."

But shortly after, as the service ended, Galina Loseva broke down, hugging the caskets.

Throughout the church service and during almost all of the graveside services, there was no mention of the boys' father.

But one of the last people to stand and speak, an old friend of Galina Loseva's, could not resist telling the crowd how much she loathed Vasily Losev.

"I know you should not talk about the dead," said Anna Saltykova, who met Galina in Yalta 20 years ago. "But he was very terrible, very hard. When he drank, he was vicious. Their life together was miserable. But she never said anything bad about him."

Ivaschenko, the neighbor, lives a block away from the apartment where the boys died. He talked about seeing them during the recent holidays.

"I knew these precious kids, so clever, so nice, so mature," he said. He gave each a toy for Christmas. "They didn't get to play with those toys very long."

Alexey (age 9) Left, Alexander (age 6) Right,
Peter (age 2) Middle – December 1998

Life Lesson 9 – Eternal Hope

At some point in the days that followed my children's deaths, someone sent me a copy of a poem called *Footprints*. This poem ministered to me in powerful ways.

When I was under the rubble of my heaviest sorrow, God carried me in His loving arms. When I was my weakest, He filled me with the peace of His presence and took my burdens into His own heart. At my greatest point of need, God's touch was like a healing balm on my wounded heart. When pain threatened to steel my very breath, the beauty of His Holy Spirit breathed into my soul like a life-affirming, balmy breeze.

Many reading this chapter will marvel that I survived such catastrophic pain. But sorrow and grief visit all lives, to one degree or another. My heart was broken many times over; yet, once a heart breaks, further damage is, in many ways, simply redundant. A broken heart is a broken heart. Something fractured and splintered can hardly become more broken. Though the extent of my loss may seem alien to your experience, I am certain, at some point in your life, heartbreak has left your own heart in shreds.

There really is no question whether or not any of us will suffer loss, pain, and sorrow. It will come. The only question is how we will respond. Will we react as though we "have no hope" (1 Thessalonians 4:13)? Will sorrow overtake and defeat us? Or will we believe in God's limitless, ever-present love? Will we hold fast to the truth that "A bruised reed he will not break" (Isaiah 42:3; NKJV)?

No matter what tribulation befalls you, you must never allow circumstance to alter your view of God. He is love. He is truth. His is the only true justice. Though your mind may struggle to understand the 'whys' and 'hows' of the turmoil you face, you must allow the Spirit within you full reign of your heart so you may be "strengthened with might through His Spirit in the inner man, that Christ may dwell in your hearts through faith; that you, being rooted and grounded in love, may be able to comprehend with all the saints what *is* the width and length and depth and height— to know the love of Christ which passes knowledge; that you may be filled with all the fullness of God" (Ephesians 3:16–19; NKJV).

I have learned that only I can control where my thoughts wander. Only I have the power to choose what gains and holds my attention. If I choose to focus on the pain and chaos of life, then it is the pain and chaos that hold me captive. If I, through an act of my own will, decide to focus instead on the beauty of my Lord, then it is His glory and truth that fill my eyes and heart.

As Joshua said, "Choose for yourselves this day whom you will serve ... as for me and my house, we will serve the LORD" (JOSHUA 24:15; NKJV).

Consider this:

1. When in your life have you faced traumatic loss that threatened to steal your faith?
2. What questions and fears surfaced during this time?
3. How did this trauma affect your relationship with God?
4. Have you experienced full healing of this pain? If not, why not? If so, how?
5. What further steps can you take to wholly trust God in this situation?
6. Read Philippians 4:8. In what ways can heeding Paul's advice enable you to walk through painful trial without losing hope?

Chapter 10

Tender Hope

As I moved through each day after I lost my children, I marveled that I could still function with some degree of normalcy. But, the world felt alien and the silence of my

> **Job 14:7**
> "For there is hope for a tree, If it is cut down, that it will sprout again, and that its tender shoots will not cease" (NKJV).

days haunted me. So much of my identity had been anchored in my relationship with my boys. After nine years of being "mom," learning to relate to life as simply Galina was much like immigrating to a foreign land—unfamiliar and frightening. Daily, I returned to my Lord, asking for His strength to sustain me as I navigated this strange, lonely life.

As days turned into weeks, and weeks turned into months, I visited the graves of my children nearly every day. Though I knew they did not inhabit the little plot of earth, I felt closest to them knowing their tiny bodies were near to my broken heart. God had miraculously granted me the "peace which surpasses all understanding" (Philippians 4:7; NKJV), but the pain of loss and separation still ached deeply at my very core. Whenever I knelt beside their graves, I would recall precious moments that were sealed forever in my heart: Aleksey running into my arms; Alexander laughing up at me with sparkling eyes; little Peter rubbing sleepy eyes and reaching up for me to hold him close. How could I ever again be whole? But the answer to that question had been planted deep within my fractured heart the day I had heard the voice of my Lord and Aleksey's sweet little voice, both encouraging me not to cry and telling me that they were happy together in heaven. God had granted me a sustaining peace; the serenity and stillness that flooded my being that day continued to live in me and spur me onward. I knew in every fiber of my being that my boys were living a perfect life on the other side of eternity. They knew a love infinitely more powerful and complete than this earth could ever offer. Wishing them back into this world suddenly seemed the most selfish of desires. My pain paled to nothing in comparison to their great joy. Even though the pain of loss and grief was very difficult, I was learning to be thankful for each day and to rely on God to get me through as I slowly made my way back to life. The fact that I still lived was proof that God had a purpose for my being. I asked Him to use me according to His will. I knew I had to leave the past behind and take one step at a time into the future.

As I began this journey, Peter and I continued to correspond. I looked forward to his letters like a school girl. Bit by bit, I learned his story.

Peter Messmer had been raised in a very patriotic family. His father was a retired Army Reserve colonel and Peter and his brothers, Steve and Gerry, all served as officers in the Army. Peter graduated from Cornell University in May of 1983, the same month I moved to Yalta and met Vasily. He began his Army service in July the same year, around the time Vasily and I were already talking about marriage. Peter was assigned as a combat engineer platoon leader with the 18th Engineer Brigade and stationed in Germany. (Interestingly, my brother Alexander had served in East Germany only a couple years before Peter was there on the West German side of the Iron Curtain—the wall of communism that kept its people enclosed and barred entry to the rest of the world.)

While serving in Germany, Peter had encountered some fellow soldiers who, in his own words, were "really on fire for Jesus." Their fire ignited a desire within Peter for a deeper walk with God. As a result, he joined them in an Assemblies of God church and quickly became involved in an evangelical ministry to the many refugees who sought asylum in Western Germany. Peter told me how thousands of refugees poured into Germany from all corners of the world where there was war and political unrest, including some from the eastern bloc countries of the Soviet Union as the USSR started to collapse. These people came from every kind of religion in the world and many of them were disillusioned and starving for knowledge of the one true God and the blessings of His kingdom.

As Peter's relationship with the Lord progressed, so did his relationship with his girl back home, Elsie Hernandez. Peter and Elsie had met at Cornell a few years before Peter began his tour of duty in Germany. Elsie had a Hispanic ancestry and her exotic culture and loving, warm personality had drawn Peter to her quickly and irrevocably. Peter shared with me a little about Elsie's life. She grew up in the south Bronx, one of seven children. Her father left when she was a little girl. But her mother, Nicolasa, was a woman of amazing strength and character. She continued on, working hard to support and raise her children in a tough, impoverished neighborhood. She kept them focused on their education as a path out of poverty. Elsie and five of her siblings eventually graduated from Ivy League universities. During his last year of active duty, Peter had flown Elsie to Germany and formally asked her to be his wife. They were married on August 29, 1987, following Peter's tour of active duty in the US Army.

During his last years of service in Germany, Peter had distinctly heard the Lord call him into full time ministry. Elsie, with a loving heart and eagerness to serve the Lord, joined him in the calling and shortly after their wedding the couple returned to Germany to minister the gospel of Jesus to the refugee population. To begin their lives together ministering hope, healing, and peace to those who did not know the Lord was a blessing without measure. As the couple shared the gospel, Elsie became like a "mom' to many of the young refugees who were far from their homelands and families.

On July 29, 1988, Elsie gave birth to Eva Marie. In 1989, Elsie and Peter knew their time in Germany was over and they returned to the US to begin the next chapter of their lives. (Ironically, they left just as the "Iron Curtain" between East and West collapsed.) They settled in Peter's home village of Interlaken, NY. Peter began working as a highway engineer and they set about the blessed task of living for the Lord and raising their little girl. Over the next six years their family grew to a total of four children; Steven Alexander was born on October 5th 1990, Joshua Charles on May 1st 1993, and Jesse Israel on April 30th 1995.

From the way Peter described things, it was easy to see that he and Elsie poured their hearts and souls into their marriage and their faith. Peter had worked every summer during his growing up years on his Uncle Joe's farm where his mom's family had been raised. Peter felt an agricultural way of life was a healthy way to raise a family; it was something he wanted his own children to experience. So in 1996, Peter began a dairy farm venture with his brother Steven. When plans didn't materialize as they had hoped, Peter and Elsie decided to explore the nearby Mennonite farming community. After several months of fellowship, the Messmers decided to join the Mennonite congregation. They lived and worked together with these strong, earthy Christians for the next several years.

Finally, the isolation from society grew to be a heavy burden on the young couple. The time they spent among these plain people had greatly impacted Pete and Elsie; but in 1998, they made the decision to leave the Mennonite world behind and return to a more conventional lifestyle.

Peter told me how the difficulties presented by the many relocations and job changes in such a short time had taken a toll on their relationship. Elsie really wanted to settle down. So Peter decided to return to his career as an engineer. They bought a house in Newark Valley, about twenty miles from where my sister, Nadia, lived. Although Elsie had degrees from Cornell and Fordham Universities, she fully embraced being a "stay-at-home-mom" and even home-schooled her children for a while. After growing up in the poverty of the South Bronx she was very happy to finally have her own home and a large, beautiful yard. Peter missed farm life; but he was content with his home in the beautiful, rural setting; he had room for a large garden and small livestock projects to enjoy with his children. Peter further explained how he and Elsie were just beginning to feel settled into their routines; work, fellowship with their church family, school, cub scouts, and all of the many other activities that go with raising a thriving family.

Then strangely, in the days leading up to Christmas Eve of 1998, Peter was overcome with a somber wave of sentimental feelings that wouldn't go away. He and Elsie had agreed to keep their gifts for each other simple. So on Christmas morning as their family sat together by the Christmas tree, Peter read a poem he had written for Elsie. It expressed how their relationship was rooted in their faith, something I had hoped for in vain with Vasily.

Dear Elsie; I know this gift is not costly,
but it speaks from the heart softly;
with a whisper it says,
"I love you."

The years of our marriage are growing
And I find more peace just knowing
That you are always
loving me.

It is my continual prayer that together we will walk
In a spiritual place where only God can take us—
A place where sunshine dances on flowers of spring;
Where harmony makes our hearts ring.

Our Heavenly Father above
Beckons us forth to His Kingdom
Where forever we may behold His wisdom.

May He guide our steps together,
that they will blend in the glades of forest deep
Or in meadows where silver waters seep.

From hillsides covered with spring snow
His Hand will surely guide,
As together we work against the tide
Of all that would come against us.

What a blessing just knowing
That together we will be going
to His Kingdom Halls so sweet.

Several weeks later, on Saturday, January 16, 1999, Peter and Elsie had taken 11-year-old Eva Marie, 9-year-old, Steven Alexander, 5-year-old Joshua, and 3-year-old Jesse to the home of Peter's close friend, Roger Correll. Roger had invited the members of their church for a day of sledding and cross-country skiing on his country property. It was an action-packed, fun-filled day. Hours of sledding and skiing in the frigid air of the New York winter brought gales of laughter from everyone; it was hard to tell the adults from the children as all tumbled and frolicked in the snow. As the day wore to evening, Elsie complained softly that she was not feeling well; so the Messmers said their goodbyes and piled into the car for the ride home. It had been a wonderful day and the entire family was exhausted. On the drive home, Elsie's condition worsened. Peter and Elsie were both a bit worried and spoke quietly of their concern. The children overheard and worry creased their little brows as they crossed the miles through the winter night.

Elsie continued to feel poorly once the Messmers returned home. She felt weak, dizzy, and nauseated. After tucking all the children in bed, Peter and Elsie retired as well. In the middle of the night, Peter arose to check on Elsie. She was still experiencing flu-like symptoms and he stayed awake, watching over her.

At 5:00 a.m. Jesse awoke and began to cry. Peter soothed the little boy and got him back to sleep then went back to check on Elsie. A hideous gasping noise assaulted his ears. Elsie writhed on the couch, straining for every breath. Her body was wracked by a vicious seizure. She was ghostly pale and contorted in agony. (The seizure was actually the end stages of a full cardiac arrest due to a congenital heart condition that had gone undiagnosed and was completely unknown to Peter and Elsie. Peter later learned that the first occurrence of fibrillations caused by the condition is typically fatal.)

Peter rushed to dial 911. By then, Elsie had grown frighteningly still. Peter began frantic CPR on his unresponsive wife. By the time the rescue team arrived, Peter knew Elsie was no longer with him. Early on Sunday morning, January 17th, 1999, Elsie Messmer passed into eternity and entered the heavenly kingdom of her Lord and Savior.

Later, Peter and I were shocked when we realized Elsie passed away on exactly the same day that I saw my boys alive for the very last time!

The profoundly unexpected loss left Peter reeling, both emotionally and spiritually. Unable to process his grief, he held to it as though it were a final point of connection to his beloved Elsie. As the weeks wore on, his grief grew into a bitterness that threatened to overwhelm his soul. How could God have taken the mother of four small children? Why would a loving God deprive the world of such a remarkable woman? Why would He deny these innocent children the love of their adored mother?

Following Elsie's death, Peter's parents, Millie and Gerry, moved into Peter's home to help with the children. After a short time, the family made the collective decision for Peter to return to the farm he still co-owned with his brother, Steven and his wife Suzanne; all hoped the quiet countryside and less stressful lifestyle would help Peter process his grief.

Once again, Peter left his engineering career. And, once again, he moved his family — this time back to the duplex farmhouse at Lively Run Goat Dairy, a growing and successful farm and artisan cheese plant, taken on by Steven and Suzanne during the time Peter and Elsie were with the Mennonites. Peter joined in the business as a partner and investor and assumed the duties of farmer and herdsman for the eighty, high-producing dairy goats. Suzanna and Steve and Peter's Mom and Dad all worked together to help Peter care for the children and cook meals for them while he worked long hours on the farm.

It was during those first weeks that Peter struggled to accept the loss of his Elsie that my own tragedy became known to him. My sister, Nadia, who knew Peter, strongly suggested he contact me. She had some sense that together we each could face and conquer our profound loss.

Peter and I corresponded often and regularly conversed on the phone. I remember the first time he called. I was away at the time, so he left a message for me. I felt like a young girl when I heard his voice on my machine. I pressed the "play" button over and over again just to hear that remarkable voice. I relished the times when we could spend hours talking. My broken English should have proven a barrier to understanding; but, somehow, Peter seemed to possess some rare ability to hear what I could not say.

We spoke candidly about our grief and pain. Peter spoke about the anger and bitterness that threatened to overtake him. I told him how I felt like a lemon with all the juice squeezed out. We promised to fast and pray for one another. With each tentative step of our relationship, healing began to flow between us. God's hand was at work to enact a miracle neither of us could have dreamed.

In late summer 1999, I received a much-needed, 30-day vacation from work. I planned to visit my sister, Nadia, in upstate New York. When Peter heard of my upcoming visit, he invited me to spend part of my vacation with him and his children. I did not feel comfortable staying overnight in his home; so Peter agreed to pick me up each morning and return me to my sister's home each evening. It was a 90-minute drive each way!

On August 3, I landed at JFK in New York City. My sister, Nadia, and Peter were there to meet me. After speaking and corresponding for four months, I was thrilled to finally meet the man who possessed that remarkable voice. He stood next to my sister, smiling the brightest, whitest smile I had ever seen.

Peter's sister, Mary Kaye, lived in a small apartment on Manhattan's upper west side. We were to spend the night with her and she had planned a wonderful, late-night dinner as a welcome. We enjoyed the evening filled with fun, lively conversation. (For both me and Peter, it seemed the heavy fog of tragedy was already beginning to burn off as God's light began to illuminate our hearts.) Once dinner had ended, we wished one another a good night, for the hour was very late. Mary made Peter comfortable in the living room and Nadia and I were to spend the night in Mary's extra bedroom. To say Nadia and I slept would be completely fiction—we talked and laughed and shared tears throughout the entire night.

The next morning we bid farewell to Mary. Peter dropped me and Nadia at her home near Binghamton and returned to his family. Reconnecting with Nadia and her family was like water after an interminable drought. We spoke of my children and reminisced of precious days gone by.

Bright and early the next morning, Peter arrived to take me to his home. I can still see him standing at Nadia's door looking every bit the nervous schoolboy. He held a gorgeous bouquet of wildflowers.

In the back seat of Peter's car sat two adorable boys with shining, dark hair. Six-year-old Joshua and four-year-old Jesse looked up at me with big, brown curious eyes. Nadia commented that the boys resembled me. Little did I know as we began that 90-minute drive that we had set off down a path toward a future neither of us could have imagined that beautiful day.

Elsie, August 1987

Peter & Elsie with Steven, Jesse and Joshua (left to right) and Eva behind the boys, Easter 1998

Steven, Eva, Joshua, Jesse in Eva's Lap, 1995

Life Lesson 10 – Tender Hope

Throughout Scripture, we are admonished to hold to hope, for without hope, life ceases to be worth living. Hope is a reaching forward into tomorrow. It is an expectation of "beauty for ashes" and the "oil of joy for mourning" (Isaiah 61:3). Hope has, at its core, a strong and sure trust that God is all He says He is and that He will do all He says He will do.

Overwhelming pain can create a kind of isolated atheism in our hearts. We see all God has done for us in the past and we look forward to the day we live eternally with Him. However, in the pain-inundated now, we do not feel His presence, nor do we see the work of His hand. Our haunted, physical eyes see only chaos and our wounded hearts feel only separation from His love. Just as atheism creates a system that will fall of its own sickly weight (as with communist Russia), so will be our fall when we allow today to be swallowed by a disbelief in God's constant care.

It is at these times our faith must rise. Hebrews 11:1 says, "faith is the substance of things hoped for, the evidence of things not seen" (NKJV). Two things must precede the operation of faith: hope and testimony.

Now, hope is not simply another word for wishing. It is not a dream or a fantasy. Hope is the surety that God is in control and that "all things work together for good to those who love" Him (Romans 8:28; NKJV).

Testimony is the proclamation of truth. Deep within us, even when our worlds lie in shreds at our feet, the truth continues to stand. Rather than allow the wails of chaos around us to drown out the voice of truth that lives within us, we must set our wills to proclaim the truth of our God. When the enemy attacks, God is our refuge. When the hand of death smothers life from our souls, our God is the Author of Life. When a cloud of darkness settles heavily over our lives, we must proclaim that Jesus is the Light of the world.

Questions will rise in a grieving heart. Doubts will assail us when our worlds collapse. Pain, loss, and sorrow will cause even the strongest among us to allow our faith to be shaken to its very core.

We may ask our questions, for Jesus holds the answer to all things. We may doubt, for faith is a gift from God and He will help us in our unbelief. We may be shaken, but Jesus is the Rock upon which we stand. We may do these things, but we should never despair. To despair is to deny the faith upon which our lives are based. One who despairs has fallen deeply into the pit of an isolated atheism of sorts, a denial of the power of God. And great will be the fall if the condition persists.

Consider this:

1. How has this chapter changed your view of hope?
2. Have you ever experienced "isolated atheism" in your own life? How so?
3. Read Psalm 42. What wisdom can you gain from the psalmist's words as you attempt to operate in faith in the face of severe trial?
4. In your own words, what is the advice to be gained from Job 14:7?
5. How can you put this wisdom into practice in your own life?
6. In what way(s) has God used others in your life to help you process difficulties or trial?
7. How can God use your life experiences to help you minister effectively to others?

Chapter 11

Childlike Hope

On the drive to Peter's farm that first day, I was reminded of the summer days I spent in the Russian countryside as a child. Flowers, trees, lakes, rivers, deer by the score ... I marveled at the scenery as we drove along the winding roads from Nadia's house to the

> Matthew 18:3, 4
> "Assuredly, I say to you, unless you are converted and become as little children, you will by no means enter the kingdom of heaven. Therefore whoever humbles himself as this little child is the greatest in the kingdom of heaven" (NKJV).

Lively Run Goat Dairy. The sight that met me when we pulled into the drive was one of tranquility at its finest. The farmhouse was surrounded by gently rolling farmland and lush green forests. A large herd of goats meandered inside a neat barn that smelled of fresh hay and grain. As beautiful as any postcard, Peter's farm was like a haven from the world.

As taken as I was by the sights and sounds of the farm, Peter's children were, by far, the highlight of my first visit to Peter's home. Elsie had been of Puerto Rican descent. Her children were a lovely merging of Hispanic and Caucasian traits. Eva, the oldest and only girl, had big, green, intelligent eyes framed by long, dark hair. She was a gentle, loving little mother to her three little brothers. Eva could melt your heart with one look of her soulful, striking eyes. Steven, the oldest boy, reminded me of King David—he had blonde, curly hair, large, blue eyes that crinkled above his dimples when he smiled, and a beautiful golden tan complexion. He also possessed David's strong will and drive to succeed. He was a handful to manage but Steven thrived on the farm and was a hard working little boy. Joshua and Jesse were the babies. Wherever you found one, the other was not far behind. Joshua had inherited his mother's olive complexion and shining, blue-black hair. His dark brown eyes gazed at the world with childlike wonder and seemed to comprehend it with wisdom far beyond his years. Finally, there was little Jesse. The Puerto Rican and Caucasian traits seemed to have blended to perfection in this little guy. He had golden brown hair that fell across his forehead above soft brown eyes. His baby-soft skin glowed with an ever-present golden tan. (Peter said Jesse looked like he had been dipped in coffee, so he often called him "The Bean"). I quickly saw that all of the children were a bundle of intelligent and creative energy. Within minutes of meeting these charming, well-behaved children, they stole my heart.

That first visit to Peter's farm was laden with emotion. Tremors of misery shook my being trying to imagine the grief Peter's little ones suffered without their mother's love; waves of compassion welled within me as I looked into Peter's lonely eyes; the beautiful land that surrounded Peter's farmhouse flooded me with a serenity I had not felt since my childhood days in Russia; and my growing relationship with Peter caused anxiety and anticipation to war within my heart.

I can't recall a moment of awkwardness as Peter and his kids introduced me to their farm. There was laughter and good-natured teasing as I struggled through my first attempt at milking a goat. Peter was so proud of his farm and his kids were genuinely excited to share with me the sights and sounds of their country world. I watched as Peter showed me the process of creating cheese from the rich goat's milk. (The goat cheese from their farm was hailed as one of the best in the United States.) The kids included me in the fun as they scampered about, feeding the goats and creating impromptu games. The earthy smells of the hay fields, the light aroma of the wild flowers that grew in profusion, the roosters crowing, the birds singing, the bleating goats—this symphony soothed my soul and quieted my mind.

Rather than sacrifice the hours each day to make the drive to and from my sister's home, Peter's parents (who lived nearby) offered me their hospitality. For the next week or so, I spent each night at their home and Peter would pick me up at the beginning of each new day. It was an enchanted time. I awoke each morning filled with anticipation. I never knew what new wonder I would encounter in that beautiful place.

Peter and I both had a deep love for the incredible beauty of God's world. On one particularly lovely day, he took me to see Taughannock Falls. The natural phenomenon was formed by a large stream that plunged 215 feet into a deep ravine and flowed into the waters of Cayuga Lake; the sight was breath-taking. We walked along the creek bank for a mile up the gorge until we reached the deep pool at the foot of the waterfall; we marveled at the amazing wonders God had created. On the way back, we meandered along just enjoying each other's company and holding hands like school children. We laughed and talked throughout that delightful day. The hours flew by on joy-filled wings. All too soon, the summer day drew to a close. As dusk approached, we waded into the shallows of the creek and sat on a large, flat rock. We watched as the sky went from blue to indigo. Stars began to pepper the endless expanse above us and we laid back and became immersed in the spectacular display of God's handiwork. It was magical. Feeling more happiness and contentment than I had in months, Peter and I walked hand-in-hand to the car and began the long drive home.

We spent most of those happy days at Peter's farm with the children. We played games; we made a disaster of the kitchen as we cooked Russian and American food; we all stood around and giggled as Peter and little Jesse entertained us with their "bean dance"; we wandered through the fields and gathered delicate bouquets of wildflowers. My heart was warmed and comforted as it bathed in the sound of children's laughter once again. In the evenings, I would gather the sleepy little ones around me and sing them old, Russian lullabies. Though they could not understand the words, their little eyelids would begin to droop and, soon, all four would be sound asleep.

One evening, Peter planned a special date for us—a dinner cruise. We drove to Seneca Lake and boarded a beautiful boat with two spacious dining decks. All during the delectable meal, Peter and I struggled to carry on a conversation. Though my English had improved a great deal during my visit, Peter and I had brought along a Russian/English dictionary, which we put to good use. We giggled like kids at the looks we received from others as we fumbled through the pages trying to find just the right word. Later, we went to the upper deck and gazed out over the sparkling water. It was such a peaceful scene with stars shining above and lights from shore creating luminous waves of light across the blackened lake. We both enjoyed the quiet, comfortable joy. When the cruise was over we disembarked and walked arm in arm along the marina. Suddenly, it was as though the stars above us had joined in our happiness; the canopy of sky became a riot of color and sound as a dazzling fireworks display began. A light rain sprinkled down from the kaleidoscope sky and Peter gently placed his jacket across my shoulders. It was such a lovely evening. He was such a delightful man.

The next morning, our brief time together was coming to an end; Peter drove me to Nadia's house where I would spend the remainder of my vacation. The trip began with lively conversation; but we were both sad that our magical time was over. After a while, Peter suddenly became quiet. Then, in a voice filled with nervous tension, he said, "Galina, what would you think if our friendship grew into something more?" His question was so unexpected; I struggled to extract the meaning of his words. I replied, "Don't beat around the bush, Peter. Just ask me straight out." After many false starts and nervous stuttering, Peter finally asked, "What would you think if we were to get married in the future?" I was stunned, but managed to whisper, "I don't know. I would need to pray about it." On this wholly unexpected note, our first days together came to an end.

After I returned to Fresno, my correspondence with Peter continued with renewed fervor. We wrote long, heart-felt letters, through which we shared our continuing pain and struggles. Though my own loss no longer consumed my every waking moment, waves of grief would still fall at the most unexpected times. Yet, each time, God's peace would flood my being and my tears would soon be spent. Peter, however, still struggled greatly in his attempt to deal with the anger he felt toward God for taking his Elsie.

Though God had granted me a supernatural peace regarding the loss of my little boys, the first weeks after my visit to Peter's farm were filled with a new kind of fear—fear of walking into a new future. I feared it was too soon to leave the past behind and forge a new life teeming with unknowns. Was I ready to take on such a challenge? I feared my heart was not ready to embrace a new love. Was love even possible when my heart was in shreds? I feared allowing myself to love and mother Peter's children would be a betrayal of my own precious sons. I feared living so far from Aleksey, Alexander, and Peter's gravesite. I feared the momentous responsibility of caring for four hurting children. How could I help them find the healing and peace they needed so desperately?

Filled with far more questions than answers, I decided to be completely candid with Peter. I wrote him a letter trying to explain all the thoughts and feelings that whirled within me. I confessed that my relationship with him had grown to something far more than mere friendship; however, I could not claim to be in love with him. I explained that I had no desire to leave Fresno; I needed the support of my family and friends and could not bear to leave the graves of my little ones behind. I tried to help Peter understand that my heart was still raw with grief. I was not capable of offering him and his children the kind of love they needed. A huge part of me had died along with my children and, in many ways, I was but the shell of a person. I was simply too wounded to offer more than a pitifully limited love. I asked his forgiveness for all the time wasted in correspondence with one such as me. I ended the long letter by telling him I would be honored to continue to be his friend.

Just as I was finishing the letter, the phone rang. It was Peter. He asked how I was doing. I told him I had just written him a letter. After a short silence, he asked, "What is in the letter?" I decided it was better to speak directly to him about my concerns, rather than simply send the hurtful words through the mail. So I told him all I had written. As was so typical of Peter, he allowed me time to voice my fears while he listened attentively. Then, with great compassion, he asked that I not come to any hasty decisions. He requested that I simply pray about our relationship and ask God to reveal His plan for our future. He encouraged me, saying I was still young and deserved to love and be loved. By the time the call ended, we had agreed to fast and pray, taking the matter to God and awaiting His leading.

My prayer was short and concise: "God, you know my heart. I don't want to choose my own course. I want You to guide my every step."

Peter continued to struggle greatly with his anger toward God. He could not come to terms with his loss. Although he didn't tell me at the time, his anger had grown to such extremes that his heart and mind rejected the prayers of everyone who was praying for him, believing that those who had not suffered such a catastrophic loss could never understand his severe grief. It hurt my heart to hear of Peter's desperate state. I continually prayed that God would open Peter's eyes to the limitless love that flowed from our Father's heart straight to his. Only by knowing and accepting God's love could Peter ever be free.

Finally, God sent a series of dreams and visions to Peter and others. Through this wonderful act of God's grace, He began to touch Peter's heart.

In the first of Peter's dreams, he was driving along a desert road under an evening sunset. The road wound up a barren hill. At the top was a car repair shop; a wizened old man, the shop owner, stood nearby. The old man was overcome by an all-consuming grief. Peter asked him, "You seem so very sad. What has happened?" The shop owner replied, "Yes, I am filled with sorrow. I have only one son. I had such hopes for his future; all that I have was to be his. But my son is dying. All of my hopes and dreams for him will never come to be. I am filled with grief and I cannot be consoled." Then the man vanished, as did the hill; Peter was left with only an unbearable feeling of the man's grief.

When Peter awoke, the dream remained hauntingly alive in his mind. It impacted him greatly as he understood God Himself had spoken to him. Peter suddenly knew beyond doubt that God was personally acquainted with the pain of losing a loved one. God had sent His only Son to earth to die. He had watched as His beloved Child suffered for the salvation of mankind. God's great love was made clear to Peter's wounded heart and God's healing power began to flow.

Yet Peter continued to complain from a heart of bitterness and stubborn pride. How could God be in control when everything seemed to have fallen apart? As he was struggling with this question, he had another dream. In this one, he found himself flying through a black void, like outer space. Then suddenly, he was spinning in an orbit; at the center was a giant eye. As he spun around the eye, he felt the awesome presence of God speaking to him from Psalm 32:8 "I will instruct you and teach you in the way you should go; I will counsel you with my loving eye on you" (NIV). Again, Peter awoke knowing God was combating the lies satan was trying to plant. God was in control and would guide him along every step of his journey through grief, if Peter would only let Him.

Even after the second dream, Peter still did not fully give over his anger. In fact, he was still sinking into despondency. Then one day, a pastor named Mervin contacted Peter and asked for permission to visit. Peter agreed. Pastor Mervin shared with Peter a dream the Lord had given a woman in his congregation. In it, Peter was standing at the head of a long line of believers who had come to pray for him. One-by-one, he rejected them and sent them away. (The woman who had the dream had never met Peter. Furthermore, at that time, Peter hadn't shared with me or anyone else his thoughts about rejecting the prayers of others on his behalf.) This woman's dream was an exact picture of what was going on in Peter's heart; it really got his attention.

Pastor Mervin also shared a vision he had. He saw Peter surrounded by lions. Their vicious snarls and bared teeth left little doubt that the wild animals wanted to devour Peter. The message of the vision convicted Peter about how far he was drifting away from

God. That night, Peter prayed with this godly man and recommitted his heart to the Lord. The visit ended with Pastor Mervin praying that God would send Peter a special dream to inspire and strengthen him. Shortly after the pastor left, Peter fell into a deep and peaceful sleep. Just as morning was breaking, he found himself in a wonderful state of being—something like a vision or dream. To this day, Peter struggles to find the right words to describe the experience.

In this dream-like state, Peter was surrounded by blue sky and felt the presence of angels all around him. He could not see them, but he heard their singing. The sound was more exquisite than any music Peter had ever heard. He longed to be a part of the heavenly chorus; and suddenly found that he was given a voice like that of the angels. Peter began to sing along with the angel host until he awoke. The amazing encounter confirmed the great blessing God had bestowed upon him through Pastor Mervin's visit and he felt peace that he was now on the path to healing.

I was thrilled that Peter had found the pathway to peace. I knew it would be a long road to total healing; but I also knew God would continue to minister His love to Peter and his children.

I continued to pray about my relationship with Peter. I asked the Lord to make clear His perfect will in my life. My feelings toward Peter were not the kind a wife feels toward a husband; I asked the Lord to bring that kind of love into my heart if, indeed, it was His will that Peter and I be joined in marriage.

About this time, Peter and I had a wonderful phone conversation. At the end of the call, Peter said, "I love you, Galina." Rather than joy, his words provoked a deep confusion. After a long, tense silence, I replied "I cannot say the same to you. I am not ready. I need more time." In a quiet, sad voice, Peter responded, "It's okay. I understand. I will wait."

I still needed to know if it was God's will for Peter and me to be together, so we continued to fast and pray. One night, I asked God to fill my heart with love for Peter if it was His will for us to marry. I was willing to accept whatever God desired. (After what happened with Yuri and Vasily, I needed to be certain that my relationship with Peter was God's plan for us.) That very night, I had an amazing dream. Peter and I were in upstate New York, walking across a green field. We held hands and smiled at one another. The feeling of happiness that enveloped us seemed a nearly tangible thing. We stopped and looked deeply into each other's eyes. Then Peter placed a ring on my finger. Suddenly, we were surrounded by Peter's family—his children, his parents, his sister and brothers, all of them were there. We began walking toward a white building in the distance. I asked Peter where we were going. He told me we were walking to the church where we would be married.

When I awoke, my heart was overflowing with love toward Peter! I was stunned by the life-altering emotion that shook my being. God had enacted a miracle in my heart—my love for Peter knew no bounds! I fairly leaped from bed and my heart sang as I prepared to leave for work. I was excited about this new, unexpected path that lay before me. I knew my loving, heavenly Father would lead me each step along the way.

When Peter and I spoke on Thanksgiving Day, 1999, Peter again ended the call with "I love you, Galina."

Now I knew I could answer without reservation. I could almost feel his joy surging through the wires when I responded, "I love you, too, Peter."

The next morning, I awoke with the sun's rays streaming through my bedroom window. The melodic chirping of the birds outside seemed to harmonize with the song that played in my heart. Peace and joy bubbled up in my spirit like an effervescent stream. God had granted me a second chance to love and be loved ... and the ecstasy of being a mother again.

Peter and Galina with Steven, Jesse,
Eva, and Joshua, August 1999

Family portrait, 2009 (Back Row, Jesse, Steven, Joshua, Eva)

Peter and Galina, 2009

Life goes on, Eva's wedding to Jake Persoon, 2013

Eva and Jake, 2013

Eva and Jake's children and Peter and Galina's first grand children, 2015! (Twins Elsie and Levi, and little Jace)

Life Lesson 11 – Childlike Hope

Jesus said we must become like little children in order to inherit the kingdom. Often, when I read these words, my mind is filled with images of my little sons. Vasily and I were the world to them. This meant that their little worlds were filled with chaos and confusion. Yet, my boys always found reasons to laugh; they were able to leave yesterday behind and look expectantly toward tomorrow. No matter the problems and struggles life brought to their young lives, they never ceased to hope for the best.

When we grow to adulthood, we often lose our capacity to face life with expectancy. Somehow, the trials we face build one upon another within us until we allow fear to create a fog of distrust around all our tomorrows.

Looking back at the days immediately following the deaths of my boys, I realize fear was a constant companion. I feared life without my children; I feared losing my identity now that I was no longer "mom"; I feared facing the unknowns of all my tomorrows.

Then too, as I considered my future with Peter, I feared taking on the role of mother to Peter's children; I feared allowing myself to love again.

In both circumstances, I allowed fear to cripple my heart and disable my ability to hope. I allowed distrust and suspicion to blanket my tomorrows in doubt rather than being like a little child and looking expectantly into my future.

Jesus also said we must possess the humility of a child if we wish to achieve greatness. Humility is the ability to put the wants and needs of others ahead of self; it colors all relationships with respect and honor. Humility is the attitude of soul caused by a heart that loves. Think of the love of a child. Their love is unconditional—it remains, even in the face of ill treatment or neglect. The love of a child is without restraint—they love completely and fervently.

Yet, when trauma implodes our lives, adult Christians often react with anger and bitterness toward God. Rather than respond as a child who loves in the face of all things, we turn against the One who loves us above all. We consider we do not deserve the trial we face and shake our angry fists at our God who could have chosen a different course ... but did not.

At the heart of humility lies the absolute certainty that God is God and we are not. Though we may never understand the courses God chooses for our lives, humility recognizes He is the only One with the wisdom to make the right choice. True humility trusts in God's limitless love and surrenders to the outworking of that love in our lives in whatever way He chooses.

Consider this:

1. In reading this chapter, what examples can you find of a lack of humility before God? What were the results?
2. When have you allowed a lack of humility before God to determine your course? What were the results?
3. What are the fears you allow to steal the expectancy from your heart?
4. Read Isaiah 41:10. What does God speak to your heart through this verse?
5. Considering the ways of God's kingdom, what channels of blessing can be opened by maintaining an expectant heart?
6. In your own words, what is the power of hope?

Chapter 12

Hope Anew

God flooded my heart with love for Peter Messmer and I was completely swept away by its joy and power. Every aspect of my life was transformed by the flow

> Revelation 21:5
> "Behold, I make all things new" (NKJV).

of love in which I walked each day. I had never known the beauty of God-centered love and I couldn't get enough.

Peter and I talked about everything. We found we shared many of the same views and understandings of what it means to be "one in the Lord." We talked about the idea of "brave love" from a poem I had read years before. Brave love meant sharing the truth about our weaknesses with each other as well as our strengths, even though it is difficult to talk about such things. How incredible it was when Peter truly listened to me and honored my thoughts and convictions; how wonderful it was to experience trust and respect from this man I was to marry. It was an aspect of love I had not experienced from a man since the day I lost my Daddy. Each day, my appreciation of Peter grew; I adored him!

Peter wanted to meet my mother and ask her blessing on our marriage; so we planned for him to visit me in California. He was to fly into San Francisco on February 11, 2000, his birthday. I would meet him at the airport and drive with him to Fresno the next day. I was beside myself at the thought of seeing Peter again!

In my excitement, I arrived at the Fresno airport ahead of schedule. I had brought Peter a red rose in honor of his birthday. When I arrived at the airport, I discovered a massive rain storm had grounded all planes. There was no way of knowing how long it could take before I could board a flight to San Francisco. The airport was teeming with stranded people and I stood among them holding my rose. Frustration and disappointment welled up within me and I began to cry like a little girl. A pilot standing nearby noticed. "Why are you crying?" he asked. I explained I was to meet my future husband in San Francisco and the flight delays would cause me to miss the chance to tell him "happy birthday" and give him his birthday rose. The pilot smiled warmly and replied, "Please, don't cry. I'll be the first flight to San Francisco when the airport opens and I'll personally escort you onto my plane." It was like a fairy tale! Just twenty minutes later, I was in the air holding my rose for Peter. When we landed, the pilot smiled at me again and said, "Say hello for me to your future husband."

Peter's plane got stuck in a holding pattern above San Francisco; so I arrived ahead of him and was at his gate right on time to give him the little token of my love. God had arranged a tiny miracle for us. It was such a small detail; but He is such a big God that He cared about even this tiny facet of our lives.

After this, Peter always called me his red rose and spoke often of how God wanted him to be as a gardener to me, causing me to bloom fully into the person I was meant to be. (Since that day, roses are a reminder for us—whether in a garden, a picture in our bedroom, or a design on a household decoration.)

When we arrived in Fresno, our first stop was my mother's home. Peter felt it was imperative that we receive her blessing on our engagement. I think he was a bit concerned; but his apprehension was misplaced. My mother liked Peter a great deal and gave her unreserved blessing to our marriage.

I couldn't wait to introduce Peter to my friends and family in Fresno—the ones who had walked with me through the valley of death. They had been there for me when my life fell apart; I wanted them to also share in the incredible blessing God had ordained. Their reaction was the same; everyone loved Peter.

On Valentine's Day, Peter and I went to visit my children's graves. The thought of leaving that little mound of earth behind was tearing at my soul. But I knew God had ordained a new path for me. I stood with Peter in the cemetery and gazed on the gravesite of my children while tears streamed from my eyes. Peter held me and shared my pain as I cried. Thinking back about my little sons now had a dreamlike quality; like a precious vision of love that had been mine for only a moment in time. But God had given me a new vision and a new dream—the time of mourning had been replaced by a season of joy. Peter stood before me at the foot of my sons' graves, his eyes sparkling with the gold rays of the midday sun; he held my face in his hands, looked in my eyes, and spoke the words, "Galina, will you be my wife?"

In His infinite mercy, God had granted me the desires of my heart; even when I was unaware the desire still lived. He sent me a godly husband, one for whom I had not searched ... indeed, one for whom I had not even asked. And God gave me a new family to love and care for. God's infinite compassion and mercy overwhelmed me; and the love and acceptance of Peter and his children surrounded me. Truly, God had brought to pass the incredible riches of one of my favorite passages of Scripture. Isaiah 61:1–3 says: "The Spirit of the Lord God is upon Me, because the Lord has anointed Me to preach good tidings to the poor; He has sent Me to heal the brokenhearted ... To comfort all who mourn, to console those who mourn in Zion, to give them beauty for ashes, the oil of joy for mourning, the garment of praise for the spirit of heaviness; that they may be called trees of righteousness, the planting of the Lord, that He may be glorified."

My heart rejoiced as I basked in the flow of God's tremendous, unexpected blessing! I wanted to shout from the rooftops about the eternal faithfulness of my precious Savior. The wind of God's Holy Spirit had filled my empty sails and carried me safely through the storm of loss and grief. Now, I was being carried into God's plan for my life on waves of His infinite grace.

A couple days after Peter proposed, my family and friends organized a large dinner party in Fresno to celebrate. I will never forget the sight of everyone smiling and laughing with us; all of them needed this time of joy as much as we did.

Then it was time to end the California chapter of my life and begin an entirely new story in upstate New York. It seemed as though the miles that separated Fresno, California from New York grew longer as our hearts grew more and more connected; the thought of being separated by such a distance was excruciating. God provided the answer to even this when Steven and Suzanne offered to host me in their home until the day I would become Peter's wife. I was like a child on Christmas morning the day I received the invitation. Peter and his friend Roger even spent weeks building an additional room on his brother's half of the duplex farmhouse that would be mine until Peter and I were married. Again, God's compassionate provision astounded and humbled me. Peter helped me pack up my belongings and send them off to my new home. It was a strange feeling to close up my apartment and turn in the key. A mix of emotions tumbled about in my heart as the plane took off and sped me toward a brand new life with Peter at my side.

When Peter and I arrived in New York, we were welcomed by his precious children. Their innocent, uncomplicated view of life allowed them to embrace all the twists and turns with an unquenchable hope. Their enthusiastic greeting imbued my heart with joyful gratitude and expectancy.

Peter and I decided to have a short engagement; we set the wedding date for March 25, 2000, exactly one year after Peter penned his first letter to me. Both of us were certain of God's will for us and we were eager to begin our new life together.

The days spent planning our wedding were golden times of laughter and excitement. Peter's children joined in with joyful anticipation. Though they all still missed their mother, they welcomed me with open arms and, more importantly, open hearts. Little Joshua, who was only six years old at the time, created a paper chain with alternating black and white links, one link for each day until the wedding. At the end of each day, he would remove one of the links—counting down the days using his little creation became a family ritual as we awaited the arrival of March 25th.

Our wedding day dawned rainy and cool. At first I was disappointed, but not even rain could drown out the brilliant light that filled my heart. In some ways, the gray, misty day seemed right and in keeping with all that had transpired in both our lives. I recently read a beautiful quote from Vivian Green: "Life is not about waiting for the storm to pass, it is about learning to dance in the rain." And so it was on that spring morning—the day I would begin a new dance with a new partner. The storm had come and the downpour had threatened to drown us all; but God had put a new song in our hearts and our souls danced with the joy He rained down upon us.

I donned my wedding dress. It was a gentle, soft blue gown with a delicate floral bodice. Although Peter wanted me to wear a white gown, it didn't feel right to me. With the tragedies we had faced and the fact that it was a second marriage for both of us, the tender, sky blue seemed the perfect choice—the color of the heavens where our hope lies.

We had chosen to be married in the Apalachin Baptist Church where Peter and Elsie had been members. Although this was not the church Peter attended at the time, the congregation had walked with him as he struggled to accept the tragedy of Elsie's death. They had stood staunchly with Peter during his "night" of extreme grief. It seemed appropriate to share with them the "joy in the morning" that God had arranged (Psalm 30:5).

The time arrived for me to walk down the aisle toward my future as Mrs. Peter Messmer. I stood at the back of the church and gazed into the sanctuary. All the children stood around me; the boys were dressed in their little black suits, with white shirts and black ties, and Eva had chosen to wear a gown the same sky blue as mine. Their little faces were pictures of happiness and joy. The tiny church was overflowing with people; we had invited everyone who had walked with us as we navigated our journeys through pain and loss. The love and joy that filled that little sanctuary was nearly tangible; the Holy Spirit had so infused the very atmosphere that no one could possibly be unaware of His presence.

Peter and I agreed to make our wedding ceremony a time of praise and thanksgiving to the One who had made all things new for us. Rather than focus on either of us or create some wedding spectacle, we chose a simple ceremony in which the name of our

Lord would be lifted up. We sang hymns in English and Russian, including my favorite, *How Great Thou Art*. ("Oh Lord, my God, when I in awesome wonder" … those words seemed written specifically for us on that day of miraculous blessing.) The pastor spoke of the love of our Savior and the salvation available through His death and resurrection. It was as though the tragedies of the past had led to this time when the doors of heaven were thrown open so all could see the redemptive love of Jesus. No one at the ceremony left untouched by the incredible love of Christ.

A very crowded reception followed in the small fellowship hall of the church. As we had done in Fresno, Peter and I made the theme of our reception a thank you to our friends and family who had stood by us. God had orchestrated our lives to become testimonies of His faithful love. We were living, loving examples of the powerful truth contained in Isaiah 61:1–3—He had healed our brokenness and given us the supreme honor of declaring His glory through our very lives.

During the reception, the rain ceased and, just as the sun sank low in the evening sky, a magnificent rainbow appeared. So appropriate … so like our loving heavenly Father to give us a sign of His blessing and a symbol of hope with which to begin our lives together.

Our honeymoon was generously provided as a gift from Peter's brother Gerry and his wife Cathy; they gave us a full week in a beautiful resort in the Smokey Mountains. Spring time in North Carolina was already well ahead of chilly New York, with gushing sunshine, brilliant flowers, mint green leaves, and singing birds. Gerry and Cathy also took care of the children while we were away.

After our wedding and honeymoon, the demands of the dairy farm and taking care of my new family took over. We spent our days feeding and milking eighty goats, making artisan cheeses, and hosting tourist events. Life was very busy, but I was blessed beyond measure to, once again, know the joys of being a mother. All of us worked in the rain and the snow, under the sun and stars. Once in a while, Peter and I would find ourselves alone in our moonlit barnyard after a long day's work. There, we would steal a kiss and look to the stars. Our thoughts would stray to Aleksey, Alexander, Peter, Dennis and Elsie; and we would hold one another as memories sparkled in our hearts.

One morning after we began our new life together, Peter woke up bursting with excitement to tell me an amazing dream. He had seen an endless field of grass swaying in the breeze; and on a nearby ridge line was a row of great oak trees. He stood at the end of a row of six people facing the trees. Suddenly a storm blew in from the horizon. The winds grew strong and the great trees bent toward the line of people. One of them shouted, "Stand in faith!" But Peter ran. Then he stopped and looked behind him. A great gust blew and the giant trees snapped. One by one they fell. The six others had stood their ground and the trees landed between them, harming no one. Peter then observed the brilliant green foliage of the canopies lying on the ground. Carved in the emerald leaves he read, "God is blessing you!"

God had inspired Peter's dream as a kind of closure—a special illustration of how He had brought us through the storm and blessed us with each other. It was also a reminder that we must stand in faith during the storms of life. It was especially poignant for Peter who had so struggled with God after Elsie died.

Many years have now passed since our wedding day. There have been mountaintops and valleys, happiness and disappointments, laughter and tears. But we have built our lives together on the only sure foundation, our Lord Jesus Christ. Peter tells me often that I am the woman of his dreams; I am so happy knowing that our lives will go on and I can continue to be a blessing to him and his children.

Raising four children is a challenge for any mother; to raise children who have known the loss of their biological mother requires more wisdom than either Peter or I possess. But the faithfulness of our Lord never ceases. He has always been with us to guide us through the tough times and shower His love upon us at all times. Whenever waves of grief or floods of questions overcame one of our children, Peter and I would pray with them and tell them of the Lord's faithfulness. We tried to help them understand that our

Lord is "acquainted with grief" (Isaiah 53:3) and can lead us safely to the other side of pain.

Our love continues to grow over the years and, like every couple, we have to nurture our relationship. One winter, after we had been married for seven years, I shared my feelings. "Peter, it seems to me that we used to be so much more romantic." So we went to a restaurant and talked about our life together and he told me, "I will do my best so you don't feel that way." Several days later, on Valentine's Day he gave me a letter in the form of a poem he had written and placed in a colorful folder, with golden braids attached. The words of the poem reflected the natural beauty of the area in which we live.

To my Galina,

Love is like an exquisite wine
Produced by the twists and turns of time.
Hidden under an emerald cape,
Young new love, like clusters of grapes
Lies snuggled in the arbor of leaves;
Drawing nourishment from gnarled vines that weave

On hillsides high. Love's inspired view
Overlooks a deep valley lake of turquoise blue
And revels in the glorious sun,
Illumined by bright colors of summers hue.

As day turns repeatedly to night,
Warm sunrises caress love with light;
And dazzling sunsets illumine glowing sights.

In such summer glory,
Love revels and frolics
To write a romantic story.

But with the gentle passage of time,
Love's fruit on the weaving brown vine
Grows and matures and gives parting call
To the protective leaves that crinkle and fall.

Then exposed and ripe for all to see,
Love's fruit is ready for the harvest to be.
Gone is the warmth of sunrise sun;
All the frolicking summer fun.

Gone are the friendly green leaves,
Rippling, shimmering on cool summer breeze.

Where is loves romance
Which freely swaggered and pranced;
And under moon light and sparkling stars
Once whirled and danced?

The excitement of summer is done
And the pain of harvest has come!

Does this mean the end of love?
Can such love sadly disappear?
Is the newness of love truly gone,
Only to be replaced with echoes of fear?

What would that say of the miracle way
When love in a springtime vineyard grew
With a beginning so fresh and new?

Rain and musty soil
Are the place of Master's work and toil!
Rewriting young crazy rhyme
As it clings to the long-winding vine.

A Master vintner will mature and make ready
The young love of the carefree and heady
When grapes are picked and loaded and hauled away.

No more summer sun—no light of day.
The strong force of wood and iron
Squeezing, crushing, transforming environ.
Something is happening to love's siren.

Fruits of love, blended essence.
Something new comes in the presence
Of the crushing, transforming wine presses.

Is not Love like an exquisite wine
Produced by the twists and turns of time?

But before it comes to pass,
The darkness of aging casks is a dirge
As love waits the time to emerge.

Will the trials and pain of change ever end?
Where is my lover, my long-lost friend?

If I secretly feel with soul's tender sense,
I know that he is here with me, too,
As we transform and renew.

Our love is now blended in flowing form;
Merged and strengthened with each other's flavor.
Who can now tell which of us was once the other?

So the forces of wood, iron, and time
Have made a new love that shimmers and shines.
It fills crystal glasses with ruby red wine.

Full goblets on a table set for two
Remind me of you.
A love deeper than it was
In the vineyards when new.

It has been transformed
By the power of time;
Mature and exquisite
Like a fine wine.

I'm happy knowing it is no longer new;
But instead, it is aged, tested, and true!

Happy Valentines, to my Sweetie, now and forever!

After I read the poem, my misgivings left me. I read and re-read it page by page. Our love—this wonderful gift from God—was breathtakingly real. I asked myself, "What more could you need, Galina? It is the dream of every woman to have this kind of love. Be happy and have joy." A happiness I had never known welled up and overflowed. Peter's words were not merely words; they showed in his actions every moment of every day. Such is the heart of my beloved, my gift, my unexpected miracle.

Over the years, we have shared joys and sorrows, love and laughter, ups and downs. Peter continues to write me romantic letters, cards, and poems. The children have grown up and gone on to live their own lives. And Peter and I continue to tell our stories of a redemptive love that knows no limits. Our stories are simply the vehicle through which God can touch broken hearts and heal broken lives. I once heard that the greatest ministry is born of the greatest pain. Peter and I now realize the incredible honor bestowed upon us by our Lord. Ours are more than stories of survival; ours are stories of victory and purpose. What satan meant for our demise, God meant for His glory. With humble hearts, we will continue to proclaim:

"Trust in the Lord with all your heart, and lean not on your own understanding; in all your ways acknowledge Him, and He shall direct your paths" (Proverbs 3:5, 6; NKJV)

"For the Lord God is a sun and shield; the Lord will give grace and glory; no good thing will He withhold from those who walk uprightly. O Lord of hosts, blessed is the man who trusts in you" (Psalms 84:11, 12; NKJV)!

Our time of great tribulation is far in the past now and we continue on through life's journey as pilgrims in this world. The path of life is still not easy; the Lord did not promise us that it would be. Yet we know that He will be with us through whatever trials still await. Our hope lies not in the fleeting things of this life; it rests on what lies ahead in the Kingdom yet to come, where every tear will be wiped away. With perseverance and God's grace, we will walk together through any wilderness of trial or pain. We will forge our way through any obstacles that lie in our paths. We will continually turn our eyes toward heaven and trust in God's unfailing love. We will make it through the thorns to the stars.

Life Lesson 12 – Hope Anew

Loss. Destruction. Sorrow. The arsenal of our enemy contains all these and more. He is an enemy to all that is beautiful. He is the destructor of all that is good. He is the accuser of the innocent and the author of hopelessness and hate. To face the catastrophic results of a life ruled by this hideous enemy can cause even the strongest heart to grow faint and the sturdiest among us to tremble in weariness.

I look back at the catastrophic events of my life and the lives of Peter and our children and am struck by a different kind of grief. It is a sadness of spirit for those who face such devastation without the Lord. I cannot imagine the hopeless state of one who does not hold to the hope of eternal life.

We have all heard it said that severe trial will either make us or break us. I am convinced of the truth of this saying. When trials hit, we can choose to gird up our defenses or succumb to the pressure. It's our choice. It's our choice how we respond to trouble or suffering or doubt. I have said this often throughout this book. It is true today and it has always been true. Eve had a choice to believe God or to doubt His word. She had the choice to cling to God's truth or let her mind be swayed by the lies of the enemy. We, too, have that choice. God's Word does not cease to be true when we are overwhelmed or confused by our circumstances. God's love does not end when we cannot see the reasons for His actions in our lives. When our tomorrows look hopeless to our limited view, God has not relinquished control. He knows what He is doing. His every act is founded on and motivated by a greater love than we can fathom.

When our souls are parched and dry, He is our Living Water. (John 4:10)

When the enemy presses in hard, He is our Strong Tower and Refuge. (Proverbs 18:10; Psalm 62:8)

When darkness threatens to blind our eyes, He will be the Light of our worlds. (John 8:12)

When we are starving for love, peace, and joy, He is the Bread of Life. (John 6:35)

When satan seeks to keep us bound by pain or sorrow or doubt, He is our Deliverer. (Psalm 18:2)

When we feel lost and alone, He is our Rescuer. (Psalm 136:24)

When life ceases to make sense, He is our all in all. (Colossians 3:11)

Alexander Pope said, "Hope springs eternal." This is true when the springs of God's living water flow unimpeded through your life. When you trust Him to lead and guide; when you trust His love to be ever-present and without limit; when you trust His plan for your life, even when it makes no sense, then will hope rise eternally in your heart.

Consider this:
1. Consider Isaiah 61:1–3. In what ways has God brought "beauty from ashes" in your life?
2. If you are in the midst of a painful or dark time, how might you choose hope?
3. According to Isaiah 53:3, our Lord is "acquainted with grief." How can this truth help as you face difficult circumstances?
4. How have you experienced the Lord as Rescuer, Light, Bread, or Living Water?
5. How can remembering those times strengthen you for troubled times you may face?
6. Proverbs 3:5, 6 and Psalms 84: 11, 12 speak of trusting the Lord. Read these verses and reflect on what trusting in the Lord means to you and what it practically looks like in your life.
7. Does "Hope spring eternal" in your life? If so, how can you thank God for that Hope? If not, how can you experience this eternal, hopeful spring?

Epilogue

The Lord has walked with us as we traveled through the valley of death. He has held our hearts and our hands as we learned to see life from His perspective. He has wiped our tears, picked us up from the depths and set our feet on solid ground—the solid rock of faith in Him. The greatest lesson we learned as we journeyed back to life is the power and importance of allowing hope to spur us onward.

It required hope to leave the pain of the past behind us and journey on into our futures. It required hope to face a lifetime of tomorrows that did not contain the laughter of loved ones. It required hope for Peter and me to join our lives together when grief had mutilated our hearts. Hope rescued us and hope sustained us. The power of hope that is founded in the Lord can never be over- estimated. Hope is what took Peter and me from sorrow to rejoicing.

By the grace of God, all our children have grown into very special, kindhearted, loving, and intelligent young adults. The road we have all traveled together has not been without pain or trial. The sorrow of mourning left each of us with scars that often tend to color our responses to life. But we have held onto one another and the Lord through it all. The words of Jesus have stood as a beacon when life seemed to be more than we could carry: "In this world you will have trouble. But take heart! I have overcome the world" (John 16:33; NIV).

Several years into our marriage, Peter and I began to feel that God wanted us to share our testimonies with others who may be going through terrible times of loss and sorrow; especially those who suffer at the hands of an abuser. The desire to offer the hope we found grew deeply in our hearts. This burning desire resulted in the creation of Galina's Hope Ministries, an organization founded to reach those whose lives have been torn apart by loss and sorrow.

Over the years, we have had the opportunity to share our stories at various churches. God has used the stories of our journeys from mourning to joy to speak hope into the lives of hurting believers and non-believers alike. To watch as the Lord brings hope and healing into hurting hearts is a blessing beyond telling.

Just as Peter and I heard the voice of our Lord in our darkest hours, so He wishes to speak life into the darkness you face. Just as the Lord protected me through years of abuse, so He will shield you in His loving embrace. And just as the Lord had a glorious morning awaiting after our nights of sorrow, so He has a plan for your life to bring you a good future and a heart filled with hope.

The words of David continue to be powerful influences in my life. In closing, I would like to share with you one of the songs he wrote. If I had not suffered such devastating loss, I would not know the full beauty of these words.

"The LORD is my shepherd; I shall not want.
He makes me to lie down in green pastures;
He leads me beside the still waters.
He restores my soul;
He leads me in the paths of righteousness for His name's sake.
Yea, though I walk through the valley of the shadow of death,
I will fear no evil; for You are with me;
Your rod and Your staff, they comfort me.
You prepare a table before me in the presence of my enemies;
You anoint my head with oil; my cup runs over.
Surely goodness and mercy shall follow me all the days of my life;
And I will dwell in the house of the LORD forever" (Psalm 23; NKJV).

"Be of good courage, and He shall strengthen your heart,
All you who hope in the LORD" (Psalm 32:24; NKJV).

We have opted to include the *Life Lessons* and *Consider This* sections in this book in order to provide a way for you to glean messages of hope from our experiences. It is not our intention to take any specific theological stance or attempt to teach doctrinal issues.

We simply wish to share with you the incredible journeys that took us from despair to expectancy. Rather than just telling our dramatic story, we hope we have provided you with a tool to help you live a life of hope in the Lord.

Hold fast to hope, dear one, when life's burdens threaten to overwhelm and defeat you. "Hope in the Lord; for with the Lord there is mercy, and with Him is abundant redemption" (Psalm 130:7; NKJV).

Abundant blessings,
Peter and Galina Messmer

Made in the USA
Lexington, KY
30 November 2015